Exit Strategies T

Related titles from Law Society Publishing:

Anti-Bribery Toolkit
Amy Bell

Anti-Money Laundering Toolkit (2nd edn – forthcoming, spring 2018)
Alison Matthews

COFAs Toolkit
Jeremy Black and Florence Perret du Cray

COLPs Toolkit (2nd edn)
Michelle Garlick

Lexcel Business Continuity Planning Toolkit
The Law Society

Lexcel Risk Management Toolkit (2nd edn)
The Law Society

Lexcel Small Practice Toolkit
The Law Society

All books from Law Society Publishing can be ordered through good bookshops or direct from our distributors, Prolog, by telephone 0370 850 1422 or email **lawsociety@prolog.uk.com**. Please confirm the price before ordering.

For further information or a catalogue, please contact our editorial and marketing office by email **publishing@lawsociety.org.uk**.

Exit Strategies Toolkit

Tracey Calvert and Helen Carr

The Law Society

ISBN 978-1-78446-073-0

Published in 2018 by the Law Society
113 Chancery Lane, London WC2A 1PL

Typeset by Columns Design XML Ltd, Reading
Printed by Hobbs the Printers Ltd, Totton, Hants

The paper used for the text pages of this book is FSC® certified. FSC (the Forest Stewardship Council®) is an international network to promote responsible management of the world's forests.

Contents

Foreword

Firms trying to survive in the legal sector have to cope with many new and evolving pressures. Factors such as competition from alternative business structures, changes to the law, the continuing erosion of legal aid and an ageing population mean that increasingly solicitors are closing their firms – whether through retirement, sale or merger.

Whatever the reasons for closure, the Solicitors Regulation Authority has stressed that firms need to have an exit strategy for their businesses. In a rising number of Solicitors Disciplinary Tribunal hearings, solicitors have been fined when their firms have failed to follow the correct procedures for closure.

There are a number of processes that must be followed when closing down a firm and the Law Society advises that every firm should have a plan in place for the possibility of closure – even if there are no plans to close in the near future. Similarly, the regulatory requirements mean that several actions need to be taken to close a practice, regardless of whether there is a successor in place. This practical toolkit will assist you to do that.

The rapid rate of regulatory change can be onerous, particularly for sole practitioners who are often the senior partner, the COLP and the MLRO rolled into one. The Risk and Compliance Service was established to help firms meet their legal and regulatory obligations, and the support offered includes bespoke inhouse consultancy, webinars, e-newsletters and online features, podcasts, seminars and conferences. In collaboration with subject matter experts and Law Society Publishing we have also commissioned a series of hands-on toolkits, of which this is one.

These practical guides have been prepared with the busy practitioner in mind. They aim to help reduce the cost of compliance for practitioners by providing a useful set of reference notes, definitions, best practice tips and templates. Much of their content is informed by first-hand information gleaned through on-site risk diagnostic visits and interactions with members of the profession, and in response to practitioner requests for tools to assist in their compliance journey.

Our hope is that these toolkits rapidly become 'must-have' elements in every practitioner's compliance armoury and to this end I recommend them to you without reservation.

The authors of this toolkit, Helen Carr and Tracey Calvert, are Law Society consultants who advise clients on exit strategies. Tracey and Helen both worked at the SRA in Professional Ethics and are aware of the regulatory pitfalls of closing a practice. The Risk and Compliance Service would like to thank them for their contribution.

Pearl Moses
Head of Risk and Compliance
The Law Society

Introduction

This toolkit has been written with the sole practitioner or small firm in mind. However, firms of all sizes will find the narrative and resources useful in planning for their closure. There are also useful sections on business continuity considerations.

There are a number of free resources available to practitioners, including guidance and practice notes produced by the Solicitors Regulation Authority (SRA) and the Law Society. We have included some extracts from these resources in the appendices. This book is intended to go into more detail on the requirements for dealing with an exit event, and to provide you with practical resources to help you with this.

By using the phrase 'exit event', we are describing any decision, made for whatever reason, to make a change to the way in which an individual or their business operates within the legal sector.

This may be a planned decision with a future date in mind, such as retirement leading to an individual's exit from a business that will continue without him or her, or a decision to close down a practice. It may be a decision that has been triggered by an unexpected event, such as perhaps the inability to obtain professional indemnity insurance, the loss of a significant client or a sudden downturn in business. It may be as a consequence of a disciplinary decision or financial instability issues.

Whatever the trigger event, the decisions that follow next are crucial. The relationship with the SRA and your clients must be well managed, with appropriate and timely communications. Practicalities such as residual duties owed to clients and former clients must be handled in an orderly fashion. Decisions as to next steps, if you intend to remain in the profession or are considering an ongoing relationship with clients, must be taken with knowledge of the legal, regulatory and ethical issues.

This guide is intended to assist you with an explanation of the decisions that must be made. Each chapter contains an explanation of a key topic, and checklists, flowcharts and other aids are included both to provide clarity and to assist with demonstrating your compliance with regulatory requirements.

We appreciate that sometimes an exit event is stressful, so we include a section detailing the contact details of organisations offering additional support and resources, including an explanation of the services offered by LawCare (see **Appendix B2**). We are very grateful to Bronwen Still, the current Chair of LawCare's trustees, for this contribution.

We would also like to thank the Law Society of England and Wales for help with access to resources and to thank two individuals in particular, the Law Society's Janet Noble and Simon Hamlet, for their support. Thank you also to John Whitehouse for his contribution and support.

1 Types of exit

1.1 Who should read this chapter?

Everyone who experiences any event that has an impact on their type of practice should read this chapter to understand the regulatory, legal and commercial implications that are triggered in different circumstances.

1.2 Regulatory requirements

These are contained in the SRA Handbook 2011 and compliance with these is a mandatory obligation for all individuals who are directly authorised by the SRA, or who work in SRA-authorised law firms.

In respect of change or exit events, the following are particularly noteworthy requirements, as specified in the SRA Handbook 2011, Version 19:

- **SRA Principle 2**: you must act with integrity.
- **SRA Principle 6**: you must behave in a way that maintains the trust the public places in you and in the provision of legal services.
- **SRA Principle 7**: you must comply with your legal and regulatory obligations and deal with your regulators in an open, timely and co-operative manner.
- **SRA Code of Conduct 2011, Outcome 10.1**: you [must] ensure that you comply with all the reporting and notification requirements in the Handbook that apply to you.
- **SRA Code of Conduct 2011, Outcome 10.3**: you [must] notify the SRA promptly of any material changes to relevant information about you including serious financial difficulty, action taken against you by another regulator and serious failure to comply with or achieve the Principles, rules, outcomes and other requirements of the Handbook.
- **SRA Code of Conduct 2011, Outcome 10.13**: once you are aware that your firm will cease to practice, you [must] effect the orderly and transparent wind-down of activities, including informing the SRA before the firm closes.

1.3 Change and exit events

There are a number of different types of exit from both firm-based practice and from the profession itself. All types of exit require you to consider different regulatory and other issues, and this toolkit is designed to provide you with a summary and explanation of the relevant matters.

The following table summarises the different forms of exit with an explanation of how the descriptions are used in the toolkit.

Table 1.1 Types of exit

Type of exit	Meaning
Retirement from the profession	The decision to leave employment and cease to work as a solicitor
Retirement from a practice	The decision to cease to work in a particular firm
Sale of business	The decision to sell or otherwise dispose of a business through the transfer of goodwill, assets and liabilities
Merger event	A deal to unite two existing businesses into one entity
Insolvency event	The business has not been able to meet its financial obligations as they become due
Bankruptcy/insolvency	The legal proceedings involving an individual or a business that is unable to repay outstanding debts

Annex 1A

Potential exits

Firm closes and ceases to trade

(e.g. due to retirement, death or incapacity of a sole practitioner, or as a result of insolvency)

↑

Firm becomes an unregulated legal services provider

(e.g. a firm ceases to carry out any reserved legal activities – certain steps in conveyancing, litigation, probate and administration of oaths – and instead provides solely general legal advice and services)

← **Types of exit: ceasing to be an SRA-regulated entity** →

Firm switches regulator

(e.g. a firm authorised by the SRA ceases to be so authorised and instead becomes regulated by the Council for Licensed Conveyancers)

2 SRA regulatory issues if you are closing your firm

2.1 Who should read this chapter?

This chapter is important reading for all those responsible for the management of a law firm that is regulated by the SRA. This includes a sole practitioner, partners in a partnership, members in a limited liability partnership (LLP) and directors in a company.

The firm's compliance officer for legal practice (COLP), compliance officer for finance and administration (COFA) and the firm's reporting accountants will find this chapter particularly relevant to their roles.

2.2 Why is it important to understand the regulatory requirements?

The proper and orderly closure of a firm is a fundamental requirement of legal practice. An improper or chaotic closure could:

- put clients at risk;
- generate negative publicity;
- damage both your reputation and that of the profession;
- put you at risk of an intervention and disciplinary sanctions, which could be very costly.

The SRA Principles relevant to the issue of closing a firm are:

- **Principle 2**: act with integrity.
- **Principle 4**: act in the best interests of each client.
- **Principle 5**: provide a proper standard of service to your clients.
- **Principle 6**: behave in a way that maintains the trust the public places in you and in the provision of legal services.
- **Principle 7**: comply with your legal and regulatory obligations and deal with your regulators and ombudsmen in an open, timely and co-operative manner.
- **Principle 8**: run your business or carry out your role in the business effectively and in accordance with proper governance and sound financial and risk management principles.

These principles are backed up by the following key mandatory outcomes and non-mandatory indicative behaviours in the SRA Code of Conduct 2011:

- **Outcome 7.2**: you have effective systems and controls in place to achieve and comply with all the Principles, rules and outcomes and other requirements of the Handbook, where applicable.
- **Outcome 7.3**: you identify, monitor and manage risks to compliance with all the Principles, rules and outcomes and other requirements of the Handbook, if applicable to you, and take steps to address issues identified.
- **Outcome 10.3**: you notify the SRA promptly of any material changes to relevant information about you including serious financial difficulty, action taken against you by another regulator and serious failure to comply with or achieve the Principles, rules, outcomes and other requirements of the Handbook.
- **Outcome 10.13**: once you are aware that your firm will cease to practise, you effect the orderly and transparent wind-down of activities, including informing the SRA before the firm closes.
- **Indicative behaviour 10.9**: you have appropriate arrangements for the orderly transfer of clients' property to another authorised body if your firm closes.

Beyond this, there are other important chapters in the Code that are relevant, as follows.

2.3 Duty of confidentiality

The duty of confidentiality (set out in Chapter 4 of the SRA Code of Conduct 2011) continues even after the retainer with the client has ended (including after the client has died – in which case it passes to their personal representatives). You remain bound by this duty after the closure of your firm, and you should bear in mind these obligations when planning how you will manage the closure.

Broadly speaking, the confidential information you hold will fall into two categories: paper-based information and electronically stored information. There will be some overlap with your obligations under data protection legislation, and these requirements are discussed further in **Chapter 4**. This section focuses on the duty of confidentiality.

2.3.1 Paper-based information

The starting point when dealing with the papers and files held by your firm is consideration of the ownership of these documents – you should not destroy any original documents that do not belong to you. If these belong to clients and former clients you can return them, or seek clients' instructions as to what to do with them. If you are unable to locate the owners of the files, you can consider other options, such as arranging for another firm to take over storage of the files, or you could scan and store the documents in electronic form, again bearing in mind that original documents such as deeds and wills should not be destroyed.

Your firm's client care letters and terms of business may reserve the right to destroy a client's file after a specified period of time. If so, you can carry out this action in reliance on these provisions. If you did not provide for this in your terms of business, you may nevertheless decide to adopt a risk-based approach to the destruction of a file as discussed in the next paragraph. We include template paragraphs for you to incorporate into your client care letters and terms of business covering these issues in **Annex 4A**. While they cannot be applied retrospectively, you may nevertheless find it helpful to include them in client-facing documents going forwards.

Before returning – or destroying – any papers, you should carry out a final review of the file to identify whether there are any high-risk issues that need to be dealt with. You may also want to consider keeping an electronic copy of the file, if you do not already have one, in case any complaints or claims arise in the future. Your professional indemnity insurer may also require you to take certain steps in relation to this in accordance with the terms of your policy of insurance.

2.3.2 Electronically stored data

In terms of storage, electronic data is likely to be much less problematic. However, you must ensure that any electronic storage system is secure and enables you to maintain your duty of confidentiality to clients.

In both cases (physical and electronic storage of data), you should inform the SRA of where the information is held, and provide contact details so the SRA can pass on this information to clients who want to access their files. You can do this by writing to the SRA (for contact details, see **Appendix B2**).

2.4 Undertakings

We mention undertakings here as it is important to establish what undertakings you have given – and how many – that are undischarged at the point at which you are planning the closure of your firm, and at the point when you will cease trading.

Many case management systems have a facility for recording on which files undertakings have been given, and the wording of those undertakings. This should enable you to produce a report listing all undischarged undertakings.

For those firms that do not have this facility, and in line with sound risk management principles, such firms should have a central register of all undertakings given. Firms that do not have a central register will need to review all their open files to draw up a list of outstanding undertakings. Once you have this list you can then decide how to deal with these undertakings as part of the closure process.

2.4.1 Personal undertakings

You remain bound by any undertakings that you have given during the course of practice, even once the firm has closed. Failure to comply with an undertaking can result in disciplinary sanctions being imposed by the SRA, and could result in an order by the court for specific performance or an award of compensation.

2.4.2   Undertakings given in the name of the firm

The SRA Practice Framework Rules make it clear that an authorised body (i.e. a firm regulated by the SRA) and its managers and employees must at all times ensure that they act in accordance with the requirements of the SRA's regulatory arrangements as they apply to them (rule 19.1). This rule also makes it clear that solicitors, members, shareowners and employees must not cause, instigate or connive at any breach of the requirements imposed by the SRA. The partners in a partnership authorised by the SRA are responsible not only as managers, but also jointly and severally as the authorised body.

Following this, it falls to the managers – i.e. sole practitioner, partners (in a partnership), members (in an LLP) and directors (in a company) – to ensure that any undertakings given in the name of the firm are complied with. Depending on the circumstances, you may wish to consider whether any of the following options are available to you:

- Where it is possible, you should comply with the undertaking and seek confirmation of this from the recipient.
- Request that the recipient of the undertaking release you from it.
- If the client is moving firm, request that the recipient of the undertaking release you from it upon receipt of a suitable undertaking from the client's new instructed firm.
- Make an application to court to be released from the undertaking.

2.5 Additional regulatory requirements relevant to the closure of a practice

Beyond the Code of Conduct, the SRA Handbook contains various additional specific requirements in relation to the closure of a firm. These are set out in the following rules and regulations:

- SRA Practice Framework Rules;
- SRA Authorisation Rules;
- SRA Practising Regulations.

Key to avoiding regulatory difficulties is effecting a proper and orderly wind-down. Keeping the SRA informed of the steps you are taking and key dates helps ensure that the process goes smoothly. Use **Annex 7A** ('Firm closure plan') to work through the issues you need to consider. We also recommend that a firm includes a closure plan generally as part of its range of business risk management and regulatory compliance policies and procedures.

2.6 New SRA Handbook (expected in 2018)

Broadly speaking, the draft SRA Handbook contains very similar requirements in relation to the management of a firm. It will require, just as the current Handbook does:

- that you have effective governance structures, arrangements, systems and controls in place which ensure you comply with all the SRA's regulatory arrangements, including other regulatory and legislative requirements; and
- that all the firm's managers and employees comply with the SRA's requirements and do not cause or substantially contribute to a breach of these arrangements.

There is also a specific requirement (set out in 2.4 of the draft SRA Code of Conduct for Firms) that:

> You actively monitor your financial stability and business viability. Once you are aware that you will cease to operate, you effect the orderly wind-down of your activities.

Many of the specific notification requirements for certain events (e.g. serious financial difficulty, insolvency events or changes to information recorded in the register) have been imported into the draft Code of Conduct for Firms at 3.6. This provision requires firms to notify the SRA promptly of these circumstances.

2.6.1 Duty of confidentiality and undertakings

The proposed 2018 Handbook does not contain any changes to the duty of confidentiality and the same considerations will apply. Both the draft SRA Code of Conduct for Solicitors, RELs and RFLs and the draft SRA Code of Conduct for Firms contain specific requirements to 'keep the affairs of current and former clients confidential unless disclosure is required or permitted by law or the client consents'. These requirements are set out in 6.3 of each draft Code of Conduct.

The professional conduct duty to comply with undertakings is set out in 1.3 of each draft Code of Conduct. The definition of an undertaking, of course, remains the same as the current definition:

> a statement, given orally or in writing, whether or not it includes the word 'undertake' or 'undertaking', in the course of practice, or outside the course of practice but as a solicitor or REL, to someone who reasonably places reliance on it, that you or your firm will do something or cause something to be done, or refrain from doing something.

3 SRA Accounts Rules

3.1 Who should read this chapter?

This chapter is relevant reading for:

- all managers and owners of a firm;
- anyone in a firm who holds or receives client money;
- anyone who operates a client's own account as signatory; and
- anyone who deals with the day-to-day administration of the firm's accounts.

The SRA Accounts Rules 2011 (rule 12) define 'client money' as being 'money held or received for a client or as a trustee, and all other money which is not office money'.

The Accounts Rules make it clear in the guidance notes to rule 32A that:

- in an unincorporated practice (i.e. a sole principal or a partnership), any client money is held or received by the principals;
- in an incorporated practice, it is the company or LLP that holds or receives client money (while the members or directors will not usually hold client money, they are responsible for obtaining and, where relevant, submitting an accountant's report to the SRA).

Assistant solicitors, consultants and other employees do not normally hold client money, and this is the case even if they are a signatory for a firm's client account.

3.2 Why is it important to understand your residual duties relating to the firm's accounts?

The SRA Accounts Rules 2011 contain important provisions in relation to the holding of client money. A key requirement of the Rules relevant to the closure of a firm is that you must return any money to clients when there is no longer a proper reason for holding the money. You must also then submit a final accountant's report to the SRA when you cease to hold client money (or operating a client's own account as signatory).

If a client is transferring their file to another firm, under normal circumstances their instructions should include the transfer of any money that you are holding on their behalf.

The core SRA Principles relevant to these issues are:

- **Principle 2**: you must act with integrity.
- **Principle 6**: you must behave in a way that maintains the trust the public places in you and in the provision of legal services.
- **Principle 7**: you must comply with your legal and regulatory obligations and deal with your regulators and ombudsmen in an open, timely and co-operative manner.
- **Principle 8**: you must run your business or carry out your role in the business effectively and in accordance with proper governance and sound financial and risk management principles.
- **Principle 10**: you must protect client money and assets.

The SRA makes it clear that the desired outcomes which apply to these rules are that:

- client money is safe;
- clients and the public have confidence that client money held by firms will be safe;
- firms are managed in such a way, and with appropriate systems and procedures in place, so as to safeguard client money;
- client accounts are used for appropriate purposes only; and
- the SRA is aware of issues in a firm relevant to the protection of client money.

You should bear these in mind when dealing with this aspect of the closure of a practice.

So as a starting point, you should return any money and assets you are holding to your clients and former clients, or seek their instructions on what to do with the money. Some scenarios, however, may make this difficult, and we set out additional guidance on these below.

3.3 If you cannot locate the client

There may be a few former clients with whom you have lost contact, and you are now unable to locate their whereabouts. In line with your duty to return any money you are holding to its owner when there is no longer a proper reason for holding it (Accounts Rules, rule 14.3), you should make reasonable efforts to trace the former client.

What is a 'reasonable effort' depends on the amount of money you are holding. Basic checks you can make include:

- carrying out an internet search;
- checking the electoral roll for the area of the client's last known address;
- placing an advert in a local newspaper; and
- instructing an enquiry agent (for larger sums of money).

In all these circumstances you should bear in mind your duty of confidentiality, and it is unlikely to be appropriate to disclose details of the client's matter in any advert or to any third party.

If, having conducted a reasonable search, you remain unable to locate the client, there is provision in the Accounts Rules to deal with the money.

If the sum held is less than £500 in relation to any one individual client or trust matter, rule 20.1(j) permits you to withdraw the money from your client account provided you comply with the conditions set out in rule 20.2 of the Accounts Rules. These conditions are that:

- you establish the identity of the owner of the money, or you make reasonable attempts to do so;
- you make adequate attempts to ascertain the proper destination of the money and to return it to the rightful owner, unless the reasonable costs of doing so are likely to be excessive in relation to the amount held;
- you pay the funds to a charity;
- you record the steps taken and retain these records, together with all relevant documentation (including receipts from the charity), in accordance with the requirements of rule 29; and
- you keep a central register in accordance with rule 29.22.

If the sum of money that you are holding exceeds £500 then you need to make an application to the SRA for authority to withdraw the money from the client account under rule 20.1(k) of the Accounts Rules. You can do this by contacting the Professional Ethics Guidance Team at the SRA (for contact details, see **Appendix B2**). The Guidance Team will need to see that you have taken reasonable steps to locate the owner of the funds.

3.4 If the client owes you money

If a client owes you money, and you are holding money on account of costs generally, you should send your bill to the client (bearing in mind the general requirement that you should bill a client within a reasonable time). Once you do this you have earmarked the money for costs and you should then transfer it from your client account to your office account within 14 days (Accounts Rules, rules 17.2 and 17.3) as it has now become office money.

You should make sure that you bill the client only for work for which you are legally entitled to bill. Some firms have got into regulatory and legal difficulties by using these provisions to 'mop up' the client account and transfer money to their office account. To take client money without being legally entitled to do so results in a theft of the money and a breach of both the regulatory obligations and the law.

If a client owes you money, but you are unable to locate them in order to send them your bill, you need to make an application to the SRA for authorisation to withdraw the money from the client account under rule 20.1(k) of the Accounts Rules (see guidance note vi(b) to rule 20).

Although the SRA cannot give you approval to then pay this money into your office account, it can potentially issue the authority to withdraw the money without the usual requirement that the money be paid to a charity, which gives you an indemnity.

If this scenario applies to you, contact the Professional Ethics Guidance Team to discuss the requirements.

3.5 Ongoing requirement to submit an accountant's report

If you continue to hold client money after the closure of your practice, you have an ongoing obligation to obtain an accountant's report (or to apply for and be granted a dispensation from the requirement to obtain an accountant's report if you are not exempt but can demonstrate exceptional circumstances – contact the SRA for further information on this), and a duty to submit this to the SRA if it is a qualified report (rule 32A.1 of the Accounts Rules).

If you are exempt from the requirement to obtain and submit an accountant's report – because you are holding less than an average of £10,000, and no more than a maximum of £250,000 during the accounting period (rule 32A.1A) – then you should keep the situation under review and comply with your obligations to return any monies to clients when there is no longer a proper reason for retaining them. You should also keep full records of your calculations evidencing your exemption from the requirement to obtain a report.

3.6 Final accountant's report

When you have cleared all the money from your client accounts (either by returning it to the client, forwarding it to another firm as per the client's instructions or by withdrawing it from the client account under rule 20.1(j) or (k)), and you have ceased to operate any client's own account as a signatory, you must then submit a final accountant's report to the SRA.

Although there are now exemptions from the requirement to obtain and submit an accountant's report to the SRA, as mentioned above, these do not apply to a final report.

The period covered by the report may be less than 12 months, and the report must be submitted within six months of the end of the period to which the report relates. For example, if a firm ceases to hold client money and operate any client's own account as signatory on 31 January, the report must be submitted to the SRA no later than 31 July of that year.

3.7 Retention of records

You have ongoing obligations to retain records of your accounts and actions under the Accounts Rules, rules 29.17 and 29.18. See **4.4**, where these two rules are reproduced in full.

Please note that when you notify the SRA of the location of any remaining ⟨
files that you are holding, and how you can be contacted to retrieve these, ⌐ ⌐⌐
should also inform the SRA of the location of your accounting records.

3.8 If you change regulators or cease to be a regulated practice

The same considerations mentioned in **Chapter 2** apply if you are converting to a
firm authorised by another regulator, or if your firm is converting to an unregulated
practice.

If you will continue to deal with client matters through the non-SRA authorised
firm (i.e. a firm regulated by one of the other approved regulators under the Legal
Services Act 2007 – see Schedule 4 of the Act for an up-to-date list), then you will
cease to hold client money for the purposes of the SRA Accounts Rules at the point
just before which you become regulated by an alternative regulator. Your final
accountant's report should cover the period up until this date and must be submitted
within six months.

Similarly, if you will be ceasing to carry out any reserved legal activities (broadly
speaking, certain steps in conveyancing, litigation, probate and administration of
oaths) and you have decided to cease practising as a solicitor and instead provide
general legal services through an unregulated legal services provider, your accounting
period is likely to end on the date at which you ceased to be regulated by the SRA.

There are, of course, important client care and other regulatory obligations that are
discussed in other chapters of this toolkit and which must not be overlooked. This
chapter is concerned specifically with the application of the SRA Accounts Rules
2011.

3.9 New Accounts Rules anticipated in 2018

In 2016 the SRA consulted on changes to the Accounts Rules as part of an overhaul
of the SRA Handbook. A further consultation was released in 2017, and at the time
of writing the SRA is reviewing the responses.

We anticipate that the new rules will come into force in late 2018, and though the
final version has not yet been approved, we expect that the relevant requirements
in relation to the closure of a practice will be as follows.

The rules will apply to authorised bodies (i.e. traditional law firms and alternative
business structures that have been authorised by the SRA), their managers (i.e.
partners, members, directors or sole practitioners) and to employees (including non-
lawyer employees). So, there will be no change from the current position.

You will be required to obtain an accountant's report if you hold client money or operate a client's own account as signatory, as is the case now, unless you are exempt. The exemption will be the same, as follows:

- that all of the client money held or received during an accounting period is money received from the Legal Aid Agency; or
- the balance of client money held does not exceed an average of £10,000 and a maximum of £250,000.

Again, you will not need to submit the accountant's report to the SRA unless it is qualified.

There will no longer be an automatic requirement to submit an accountant's report to the SRA when you cease to hold client money or operate a client's own account as signatory. Instead, the SRA may require you to obtain or deliver an accountant's report upon reasonable notice, when you cease to operate as an authorised body and to hold or operate a client account.

We anticipate that when you notify the SRA of the closure of your firm (or of the transfer to being regulated by one of the other approved regulators – such as the Council for Licensed Conveyancers – or of becoming an unregulated entity), the SRA will then consider whether it is appropriate to request that you submit a final accountant's report.

4 Documents and records

4.1 Who should read this chapter?

This chapter is relevant to everyone who holds clients' files (both current and former clients), anyone who is a role-holder (an executor, attorney, etc.) and everyone who must comply with the Data Protection Act 1998 and related legislation, and – with effect from 25 May 2018 – the General Data Protection Regulation (Regulation (EU) 2016/679).

In other words, the guidance in this chapter applies to the majority of practitioners regardless of their reason for exiting a firm and/or the legal profession.

4.2 Regulatory requirements

Solicitors, and other individuals employed in SRA-authorised law firms, must comply with the SRA Handbook. In respect of matters relating to documents and records, the following requirements must be achieved, as described in the SRA Handbook 2011, Version 19:

- **SRA Principle 2**: you must act with integrity.
- **SRA Principle 4**: you must act in the best interests of each client.
- **SRA Principle 6**: you must behave in a way that maintains the trust the public places in you and in the provision of legal services.
- **SRA Code of Conduct 2011, Outcome 4.1**: you must keep the affairs of clients confidential unless disclosure is required or permitted by law or the client consents.
- **SRA Code of Conduct 2011, Outcome 4.5**: you must have effective systems and controls in place to enable you to identify risks to client confidentiality and to mitigate those risks.
- **SRA Code of Conduct 2011, Outcome 7.5**: you must comply with legislation applicable to your business, including anti-money laundering and data protection legislation.

4.3 Specific issues with client files

Client files will contain confidential information. As a matter of professional conduct, you owe a duty of confidentiality to all clients and former clients. As implied by this statement, this duty continues despite the end of the retainer and even in circumstances where the client or former client has died.

Confidential information can only be disclosed to third parties with the consent of the client or in order to comply with a legal duty (such as the reporting requirements in the Money Laundering, Terrorist Financing and Transfer of Funds (Information on the Payer) Regulations 2017, SI 2017/692). Lack of suitable arrangements for the storage and destruction of files may result in a breach of this duty.

In terms of storage, confidentiality duties run alongside a professional responsibility to the owner of documentation on client files. The documentation that belongs to you and the firm can be stored and destroyed in accordance with your own internal policies, although bear in mind the need to consider whether it is prudent to retain documents/information in respect of claims and other issues that you may need to deal with.

There will also be documentation on client files that does not belong to you. The fact that you are storing such documents means that you have obligations to keep the papers safe and not destroy them unless you have the consent of the documentation owner. Loss or unauthorised destruction is likely to give rise to professional responsibility concerns. Some documentation should not be destroyed, e.g. original wills and trust documents.

In addition, client files and other records that are in your possession may identify data subjects to whom you owe legal obligations to keep their data safe and secure. Data subjects can be clients and third parties. The rights of data subjects are protected by statute, enforced by the Information Commissioner's Office, which means failure to comply may lead to legal liability issues as well as creating regulatory issues.

4.4 Specific issues relating to your own records: requirements arising from the SRA Handbook

Every business will have many requirements to make and keep records relating to the entity.

For a law firm it is important to bear in mind that while many of your record-keeping duties concern client matters, there are additional regulatory requirements in the SRA Handbook in respect of certain business-related records that you must keep for defined periods of time, regardless of whether or not the firm closes during that period. Here are some examples.

From the SRA Accounts Rules 2011:

> **Retention of records**
>
> 29.17 You must retain for at least six years from the date of the last entry:
>> (a) all documents or other records required by rule 29.1 to 29.10, 29.12, and 29.15 to 29.16 above;

(b) all statements required by rule 29.11(a) above and passbooks, as printed and issued by the bank, building society or other financial institution; and/or all on-line records obtained and saved in electronic form under rule 29.11(b) above, for:

   (i)   any general client account or separate designated client account;
   (ii) any joint account held under rule 9;
   (iii) any account which is not a client account but in which you hold client money under rule 15.1(a) or rule 16.1(d); and
   (iv) any office account maintained in relation to the practice, but not the office accounts of an MDP operated solely for activities not subject to SRA regulation;

(c) any records kept under rule 8 (liquidators, trustees in bankruptcy, Court of Protection deputies and trustees of occupational pension schemes) including, as printed or otherwise issued, any statements, passbooks and other accounting records originating outside your office;

(d) any written instructions to withhold client money from a client account (or a copy of your confirmation of oral instructions) in accordance with rule 15;

(e) any central registers kept under rule 29.19 to 29.22 below; and

(f) any copy letters kept centrally under rule 28.2 (dividend cheques endorsed over by nominee company).

29.18 You must retain for at least two years:

(a) originals or copies of all authorities, other than cheques, for the withdrawal of money from a client account; and

(b) all original paid cheques (or digital images of the front and back of all original paid cheques), unless there is a written arrangement with the bank, building society or other financial institution that:

   (i) it will retain the original cheques on your behalf for that period; or
   (ii) in the event of destruction of any original cheques, it will retain digital images of the front and back of those cheques on your behalf for that period and will, on demand by you, your reporting accountant or the SRA, produce copies of the digital images accompanied, when requested, by a certificate of verification signed by an authorised officer.

(c) The requirement to keep paid cheques under rule 29.18(b) above extends to all cheques drawn on a client account, or on an account in which client money is held outside a client account under rule 15.1(a) or rule 16.1(d).

(d) Microfilmed copies of paid cheques are not acceptable for the purposes of rule 29.18(b) above. If a bank, building society or other financial institution is able to provide microfilmed copies only, you must obtain the original paid cheques from the bank etc. and retain them for at least two years.

From the SRA Financial Services (Conduct of Business) Rules 2001 (the following records must be kept for six years):

Rule 5: Records of transactions

5.1 Where a firm receives instructions from a client to effect a transaction, or makes a decision to effect a transaction in its discretion, it shall keep a record of:

    (a) the name of the client;
    (b) the terms of the instructions or decision; and
    (c) in the case of instructions, the date when they were received.

5.2 Where a firm gives instructions to another person to effect a transaction, it shall keep a record of:

    (a) the name of the client;
    (b) the terms of the instructions;
    (c) the date when the instructions were given; and
    (d) the name of the other person instructed.

...

Rule 6: Record of commissions

6.1 Where a firm receives commission which is attributable to regulated activities carried on by the firm, it shall keep a record of:

    (a) the amount of the commission; and
    (b) how the firm has accounted to the client.

4.5 Specific issues relating to your business affairs

There is also a legal requirement to retain other records and documents, such as those connected with your own financial position, the firm's value added tax and other taxation records.

The firm's accountants can provide further assistance on the records that must be kept. Guidance is also available online at **www.gov.uk**.

4.6 Documents and records checklist

For all these reasons, when exiting a firm or practice there are a number of issues to consider relating to documents and records. The following table flags some key points.

Table 4.1 Documents and records checklist

Question	Compliance thoughts	Audit trail (to be completed by firm)
What client files are in our possession?	Do we have up-to-date lists of all the files that are in our storage or archive systems?	
What evidence do we have about the information we gave to clients about file storage and destruction?	Do we have evidence of what we told our clients at the end of the retainer? Have we complied with our internal policy and with what we agreed with our clients?	

Question	Compliance thoughts	Audit trail (to be completed by firm)
Can we safely destroy any client files? Some firms have a destruction policy and reserve the right to destroy files after a specified period of time. This may be contained in either the terms of business or agreed with the client at the end of the matter.	Do we have sufficient evidence that the client/document owner is aware of the data we hold and our policy about destruction? Does our storage and destruction system entitle us to destroy files after a certain period, and have we complied with this? Alternatively, can we return any paperwork to the client? What records should we keep about the files we have returned or destroyed?	
Have we identified documents on file that must be preserved? For example, original wills should not be destroyed.	How do we record these documents? What have we said to the document owners about ongoing storage?	
If we are merging with another firm, what files will they store?	Do we have an agreed list of files that will be transferred on a merger? What information have we provided to clients about the changed location of their files/ documents?	
On retirement, what arrangements have we made for the continuing safe storage of files?	Do we have safe storage facilities and lists of files? Have we notified clients about how they can retrieve their files?	
Have we notified the SRA of the location of client files?	Have we advised the SRA about ongoing storage arrangements?	

4.7 Further resources

For further information on this area, see the Law Society practice notes:

- File Closure Management
- File Retention: Trusts
- Who Owns the File?

at **www.lawsociety.org.uk/support-services/advice/practice-notes.**

Annex 4A

Storage of papers and documents: statement to include in terms and business literature

After completing any work, we are entitled to keep all papers and documents while there is money owing to us for our charges and expenses.

Where stored, a file of papers is kept in storage for not less than six years. After that, storage is on the clear understanding that we have the right to destroy papers after such period as we consider reasonable, or to make a charge for storage if we ask the clients to collect the papers and they fail to do so.

We will not destroy any documents such as wills, deeds and other securities, which we have been asked to hold in safe custody. No charge will be made for such storage unless prior notice in writing is given of a charge to be made from a future date, which may be specified in that notice.

If we retrieve papers or documents from storage in relation to continuing or new instructions to act, we will not normally charge for such retrieval. However, we will normally make a charge based on time spent for producing stored papers or documents to the client or to another party at the client's request.

5 Specific considerations for different types of practices

5.1 Who should read this chapter?

This chapter highlights particular issues for different types of law firms. The chapter is particularly helpful if you are a sole practitioner or are in a partnership. This chapter will also help you to plan ahead and to take account of various factors for inclusion in your firm's business continuity plan.

5.2 If you are a sole practitioner

Planning for the closure of your firm if you are a sole practitioner presents its own unique issue: who will step in to manage the practice and close it properly if you are suddenly incapacitated – or if you die?

You should consider this question well in advance, and make provision for an appropriate person to deal with your practice in such circumstances, to avoid the need for the SRA to intervene. Interventions can be costly and the SRA may seek to recover the cost of this from your estate.

Some sole practitioners already have a mutual agreement with another sole practitioner in their area to provide an independent complaints handling function for their firm (subject, of course, to a client's consent). This arrangement could be extended to cover the closure of the firm in the event of incapacity or death.

Alternatively, you may have a trusted member of staff, or a deputy COLP or COFA, who could manage the closure of the practice. Details of this individual, and the information he or she will need to deal with the closure properly, should be set out in your closure plan.

Finally, you may want to appoint a non-solicitor family member to deal with matters in the event of your incapacity or death.

If you choose this option you should ensure that you provide detailed guidance and information in your closure plan to enable the appointee to properly manage the closure, and to avoid the need for the SRA to step in (with the inevitable costs this will incur). Any appointments should be reflected in the terms of your will, and you should ensure that your will is kept up to date.

The SRA Authorisation Rules 2011, rule 25.5 requires that the SRA is notified within seven days of the death of a sole practitioner. The rule also provides that within 28 days of the death an emergency application may be made, on the prescribed form, for recognition as a recognised sole practice by a solicitor (or registered European lawyer (REL)) who is:

- the sole practitioner's executor;
- a practice manager appointed by the sole practitioner's personal representatives; or
- an employee of the firm.

If the emergency application for recognition is granted, recognition is deemed to run from the date of death; recognition will cease to have effect on the winding up of the estate *or* 12 months from the date of death, whichever is the earlier.

5.3 If you are in a partnership

Although contingency and business continuity planning is somewhat easier for a partnership than for a sole practitioner, there are nevertheless important regulatory issues to bear in mind.

If you are a partnership of two individuals, you should consider carefully what you will do if one of the partners becomes incapacitated or dies. Particular regard should be had to the requirements of the SRA Authorisation Rules.

For example, if one of the partners in a two-partner firm becomes the subject of a specified event (e.g. is committed to prison, becomes incapacitated, abandons the practice or is made subject to a condition on his or her practising certificate that prevents him or her from continuing as a partner), the remaining partner must inform the SRA within seven days of this happening.

The remaining partner will then need to apply for temporary emergency recognition to continue practising and to enable him or her to apply to be a recognised sole practitioner, or to otherwise remedy the inevitable breach of the terms of the authorisation that will have occurred. A key requirement is that the event must not have been reasonably foreseeable.

These provisions are set out in rules 24 and 25 of the SRA Authorisation Rules 2011.

5.4 LLPs and limited companies

Similar rules apply in respect of LLPs and limited companies – there are provisions to enable a firm to apply for temporary emergency recognition if various circumstances render the firm in breach of its terms of authorisation. Again, there is a requirement that the event must not have been reasonably foreseeable.

5.5 Draft SRA Handbook 2018

The draft SRA Authorisation of Firms Rules set out the provisions relating to temporary emergency authorisation or approval, and are similar in application to the current rules.

Rule 15.1 applies:

- to an application for temporary emergency authorisation of a firm where any change in the management of control of an authorised body brings into being a new unauthorised body or practice (you must apply within seven days);
- to an application needing to be made on the death or incapacity of a sole practitioner (you must apply within 28 days); and
- to an application for temporary emergency approval of a compliance officer (you must apply within seven days).

Again, the draft Rules make it clear that the SRA will only grant an application if:

it is satisfied that ... the body or its managers could not reasonably have commenced a substantive application for authorisation under Part 2 in advance of the events giving rise to the application.

6 Insolvency

6.1 Who should read this chapter?

Anyone involved in the financial management of a firm that may be in financial difficulty should read this chapter. There is also important information for individuals who have financial problems.

A fundamental requirement is that if you and/or your firm are in financial difficulties you must notify the SRA of this. You can contact the SRA at the address at **Appendix B2**. You have an obligation to make this notification under Outcome 10.3 in the SRA Code of Conduct 2011.

6.2 Personal bankruptcy

If you will be personally bankrupt, it is essential that you notify the SRA of this as soon as possible. In any event, you must inform the SRA within seven days of you being made the subject of bankruptcy proceedings (regulation 15.1(c) of the SRA Practising Regulations 2011).

In addition to this, s.15(1) of the Solicitors Act 1974 automatically suspends any practising certificate when the holder is declared bankrupt. You can apply to the SRA to have this suspension lifted by writing to the address listed at **Appendix B2**.

6.3 Corporate insolvency

Again, if it is likely that your firm will become insolvent, or if it is suffering financial difficulties, you must notify the SRA of this as soon as possible. The SRA Practice Framework Rules 2011 require you to notify the SRA within seven days if a 'relevant insolvency event' occurs.

A relevant insolvency event for these purposes occurs if:

    (i)   a resolution for a voluntary winding up of the body is passed without a declaration of solvency under section 89 of the Insolvency Act 1986;

    (ii)   the body enters administration within the meaning of paragraph 1(2)(b) of Schedule B1 to that Act;

    (iii) an administrative receiver within the meaning of section 251 of that Act is appointed;

    (iv) a meeting of creditors is held in relation to the body under section 95 of that Act (creditors' meeting which has the effect of converting a members' voluntary winding up into a creditors' voluntary winding up);

    (v)   an order for the winding up of the body is made;

(vi) all of the managers in a body which is unincorporated have been adjudicated bankrupt; or

(vii) the body is an overseas company or a *societas Europaea* registered outside England, Wales, Scotland and Northern Ireland and the body is subject to an event in its country of incorporation analogous to an event as set out in paragraphs (i) to (vi) above.

SRA Handbook Glossary 2012

7 Notifying relevant parties

There are many people and organisations who either must be informed of your decision and the closure of the firm, or will find it helpful to know of your decision. This chapter is designed to help you identify both types of contacts.

7.1 Who should read this chapter?

Everyone to whom a change or exit event is relevant must read this chapter. Your exit will be marred if your notification responsibilities are not handled correctly.

This chapter provides details of those individuals and bodies that must be told of your changed circumstances, and also provides suggestions as to others who may find it helpful to be told.

7.2 Regulatory requirements

As specified in the SRA Handbook 2011, Version 19:

- **SRA Principle 7**: you must comply with your legal and regulatory obligations and deal with your regulators and ombudsmen in an open, timely and co-operative manner.
- **SRA Code of Conduct 2011, Outcome 10.13**: once you are aware that your firm will cease to practise, you effect the orderly and transparent wind-down of activities, including informing the SRA before the firm closes.

7.3 Mandatory requirement to notify the SRA

You must comply with Outcome 10.13 of the SRA Code of Conduct 2011 if you decide to close your practice. Closure also extends to any merger-based scenario.

The notification to the SRA must usually be prior to the date of cessation so that the SRA can be satisfied on all matters relating to orderly closure and client protection.

You need to notify the regulatory Notifications Team in one of the following ways:

- By letter: addressed to the Notifications Team, Solicitors Regulation Authority, The Cube, 199 Wharfside Street, Birmingham, B1 1RN/DX 720293 Birmingham 47
- By email: **notifications@sra.org.uk**
- By contacting the firm's supervisor if he or she is known to you.

The form of notification must include the following information:

- The name of the firm, any trading names and practising address.
- The date on which the firm will cease to practise.
- The reason for closure.
- A request to revoke the firm's authorisation – or recognition as a sole practitioner, as the case may be – from the date of closure.
- Where client files and documents will be stored.

After the initial notification, you are obliged to keep the SRA updated as to any changes in your circumstances – such as if the date of closure changes – and to deal with any enquiries which it may have in an open, timely and cooperative way.

7.4 Current clients of the firm

You must inform all clients for whom you currently act, giving them as much notice as possible to ensure that their matters are not put at risk.

It is customary to have arrangements with another firm (either the firm with whom the business is merging or another firm) for the transfer of live matters. However, clients must be in a position where they are able to make an informed decision as to how they wish to proceed. Freedom of choice is important, and you should ensure that you have evidence that you have sought instructions.

The information that you give your clients must include the following:

- The date of closure.
- Whether the closure will lead to a merger of the practice with another law firm. If the firm is being sold as a going concern, this information should also be communicated, together with a request for the client's instructions as to the transfer of their file to this new practice.
- Details of the matters that are still to be performed, their options as to legal representation and a request for the client's instructions.
- Details of any client monies held by the closing firm, with a request for instructions.
- Information about any trustee or similar positions held by members of the closing practice.

Your own professional conduct duties may be put at risk if your clients are not informed of the closure. For example, there may be scrutiny of your confidentiality duties and the outcomes connected with client care, plus your compliance with the SRA Accounts Rules 2011.

However, if obtaining client consent is not possible because of the urgency of your circumstances (for example, if there is a risk that your premises will be repossessed, and file security put in doubt), you should consider the merits of transferring files to another SRA-authorised law firm without obtaining your clients' prior agreement. In such circumstances, the new firm must contact the clients as soon as possible and seek consent.

7.5 Former clients of the firm

It is good practice to contact former clients of the firm with whom the business, and individuals within it, have an ongoing relationship. This may be because the firm is holding deeds, wills and other original documents, or because individuals are role-holders such as executors, trustees, etc.

It is advisable that in such circumstances you tell the former clients where their files and original documents will be stored. It is also necessary to consider the appropriateness, and the regulatory considerations, of continuing to fulfil your role. For further information, please see **Chapter 10**.

7.6 Your staff

Part of the regulatory expectation that arises in connection with orderly closure arrangements includes the need to consider employment-related issues such as staff notice and redundancy processes.

It would be considered unprofessional – and very likely not indicative of SRA Principle 8 and the requirement for proper governance – if staff and business-related matters are not factored into your closure arrangements.

For more information, see the redundancy consultation page on the government's website (at **www.gov.uk/staff-redundant/redundancy-consultations**) and the ACAS website (at **www.acas.org.uk**).

7.7 Checklist of other bodies to notify

You also need to consider other organisations who must know of your decision.

These may include the following:

- your accountants;
- your bank/building society;
- companies or LLPs using your office as a registered address;
- counsel's chambers;
- court offices/court records;
- the Crown Prosecution Service/police;
- directories and similar (e.g. professional/telephone);
- the Information Commissioner (data protection);
- introducers with whom you have an arrangement;
- HMRC;
- the Land Charges Registry (key number);
- your landlord;
- the Land Registry (regarding current matters);
- the Legal Aid Agency;
- your local authority (regarding business rates);
- the *London Gazette* and one other newspaper (not necessary for mergers);
- mortgage lenders where you are on the panel.

Annex 7A
Firm closure plan

Introduction

This is the closure plan for [*firm name*] and will be followed in the event that the firm ceases trading. It sets out key actions and requirements and provides important contact information where relevant.

The manager(s) of the firm (i.e. the sole practitioner, the partners, the members or the directors) are responsible for this plan.

It will be reviewed annually and the latest version will be stored [*detail location*].

[Additional paragraph to include for sole practitioners, and for companies with only one director:

In the event of the death or incapacity of [*name of sole practitioner*], this plan should be passed to [*name of appointed solicitor manager*] to facilitate the orderly wind-down of the practice. [*Name*] will be appointed as the solicitor manager [under sole practitioner's will/by sole practitioner's personal representatives/under a lasting power of attorney].]

Notifying the SRA

1. We will notify the SRA of our decision to close the practice as soon as possible, and in any event within seven days of the decision being made.
2. We will do this by writing to the SRA at [*address*] and by email to [*address*] using the template form of notification at [*Appendix X*].
3. We will notify the SRA of our reason for closure, the date of closure and request that our authorisation be revoked.
4. If necessary, an application for temporary emergency recognition will be made. This will be done by writing to the SRA at the above address.

Other regulatory issues

1. Undertakings

   (a) We will produce a list of outstanding undertakings at the date of closure by [*detail method for doing this*].
   (b) Where possible, we will comply with the outstanding undertakings and obtain confirmation of this from the recipients.
   (c) If clients are transferring files to other firms, we will discuss with the clients' new firms the possibility of providing a satisfactory undertaking to the recipient in order for us to obtain a release from our undertakings.

(d)   We will consider whether the wording of any undertakings we have given means that we need to take additional steps to protect our position, and whether we should exercise any lien over clients' documents or assets. This will only be used as a last resort, and only where in all the circumstances it is reasonable for us to take this action.

2. Accounts Rules compliance

(a)   We will continue to comply with our obligations under the SRA Accounts Rules throughout and after the closure of the firm.

(b)   We will return any outstanding monies to clients or third parties, or we will transfer the funds to alternative firms instructed by clients. We will of course bear in mind our obligations under the Money Laundering Regulations 2017 and other relevant legislation in doing this.

(c)   When we have ceased to hold all client money, and operate a client's own account as signatory, we will instruct [*accountant name*] to prepare a final accountant's report.

(d)   We will submit this report to the SRA within six months of the date on which we ceased to hold client money or operate a client's own account as signatory.

Informing clients

1.   We will produce a list of the firm's current clients, and a list of any former clients for whom the firm is storing assets or documents, so that we can notify them of our decision to cease practising. [*Detail how to produce the list.*]

2.   We will give clients as much notice as possible in order to facilitate the transition of clients' files to alternative legal representatives.

3.   We will clearly set out the date of closure and will explain the options available to clients. We will use the template letter in [*Appendix X*] to do this.

4.   We will prioritise those clients whose matters are urgent.

Informing third parties

1.   We will review the firm's list of open matters to ascertain which other third parties should be informed of the firm's decision to close.

2.   In addition to this, we will notify all people listed in [*Appendix X*].

3.   We will write to each relevant third party's address, and, if we have an email address, we will contact them by email.

4.   We will use the template letter in [*Appendix X*] to do this.

Client files and assets

1.   In preparation for the closure of the firm we will compile a list of paper documents and electronically stored information.

2. We will establish whether we can return paper documents to the owner or destroy them. We will scan and maintain an electronic copy of these paper documents. We will not destroy any original documents, such as deeds or wills.
3. If we need to retain any paper documents, such as deeds or wills, we will arrange for secure and confidential storage of these documents at [*address/ location*]. [*Name*] will be the person responsible for this and will provide [his/ her] details to the SRA as part of the closure notification in case these documents need to be accessed by the SRA or other third parties, including clients.
4. We will inform any clients for whom we will continue to hold documents how they can access these documents when the firm is closed. This will be done in the client notification letter listed above.
5. We will arrange an appropriate postage forward-on facility to maintain client confidentiality when we vacate our premises, and to ensure that we can comply with any requests for client files and documents.

Professional indemnity insurance

1. We will notify our professional indemnity insurer [*insurer name*] and broker [*broker name*] of the decision to close.
2. [Successor practice [*detail successor practice*].] or [As the firm will not have a successor practice, we will pay for run-off cover in accordance with the terms of our professional indemnity insurance.]

Assets of the practice

1. [*Name*] will be responsible for ensuring that all assets of the practice are collected in and appropriately dealt with. These include electronic devices and other physical hardware.
2. All electronic assets containing confidential information will be carefully managed to ensure that this information is protected. When necessary, these assets will have the information properly and securely removed, and the device appropriately digitally cleansed.

Publicity

1. [*Name*] will be responsible for appropriately publicising the closure of the firm. This includes posting the relevant notices, managing the firm's electronic communications, and using appropriate signage at the firm's premises.
2. We will update our stationery to make it clear that the firm is no longer trading.

Review

This plan will be reviewed annually by [*name*].

Signed...

Date ....

Annex 7B
SRA notification requirements checklist

Delete as appropriate, depending on the circumstances.

Requirement	Rule/Regulation	Time limit	Date completed	Signed
To notify the SRA of the firm's decision to close	Outcome 10.13, SRA Code of Conduct 2011	As soon as possible and, in any event, within seven days of [date]		
To notify the SRA if a relevant insolvency event has occurred or if an individual has become bankrupt or entered into an individual voluntary arrangement	Rule 18.4, SRA Practice Framework Rules 2011; rules 15.1(c) and (d), SRA Practising Regulations 2011	Within seven days of the event occurring		
To notify the SRA if a sole practitioner has died or otherwise become incapacitated, is committed to prison in civil or criminal proceedings, or is made subject to a condition on his or her practising certificate or registration which would be breached by continuing to be a sole practitioner	Rules 8.7 and 25.5, SRA Authorisation Rules 2011; rules 15.1(c) and (d), SRA Practising Regulations 2011	Within seven days of the event occurring		
To notify the SRA if one partner in a two-partner firm has died or become incapacitated, is committed to prison in civil or criminal proceedings, or is made subject to a condition on his or her practising certificate or registration which would be breached by continuing to be a manager of the body	Rules 8.8, 8.9 and 8.10, SRA Authorisation Rules 2011	Within seven days of the event occurring		
To notify the SRA if the sole director in a company has died or become incapacitated, is committed to prison in civil or criminal proceedings, or is made subject to a condition on his or her practising certificate or registration which would be breached by continuing to be a manager of the body	Rules 8.8, 8.9 and 8.10, SRA Authorisation Rules 2011	Within seven days of the event occurring		

Requirement	Rule/Regulation	Time limit	Date completed	Signed
To notify the SRA if one of the members of an LLP comprising only two members dies or becomes incapacitated, is committed to prison in civil or criminal proceedings, or is made subject to a condition on his or her practising certificate or registration which would be breached by continuing to be a manager of the body	Rules 8.8, 8.9 and 8.10, SRA Authorisation Rules 2011	Within seven days of the event occurring		
To notify the SRA, and supply the SRA with a contact address, if a solicitor, registered European lawyer or registered foreign lawyer ceases to practise	Rule 15.2, SRA Practising Regulations 2011	Within seven days of the event occurring		
To notify the SRA if an authorised body becomes aware of any change to relevant information about itself, its employees, managers or interest holders, including any non-compliance with the SRA Authorisation Rules 2011 and the conditions on the body's authorisation	Rule 8.7(c), SRA Authorisation Rules 2011	As soon as the authorised body becomes aware of the change		

Checklist template

Party	Date	Acknowledged/further correspondence needed

Annex 7C

Draft letter of notification to the SRA

I am the owner/a partner/a director/a member of [*firm name*], which is a law firm authorised by the SRA under registration number [*number*].

I/we practise from [*list all offices*] and use the following trading names: [*add all trading names*].

We write to inform you that I/the partners/the directors/the members of this firm have decided to close this firm with effect from [*date*].

The reason for the closure is [*give reason*].

Please will you arrange for the revocation of [*my recognition as a sole practitioner/ the firm's authorisation*] from the date of closure.

I/we have contacted all current and former clients to advise them of my/our decision.

[The firm has been sold to/is merging with [*firm name*] which practises from [*firm address*].]

Client files and documents will in future be stored at [*location*]/All client files and documents will be transferred to [*firm name/location*] on [*date*] unless we receive clients/former clients' instructions to return their files to them or transfer them to another firm.

We will keep you updated should any of the above arrangements change.

Yours faithfully

[*Signed*]

Annex 7D

Current client checklist

Client/File reference	What work must be done to complete retainer	Has client been notified of firm closure?	Has client responded?
Brief description of client/type of work/when file opened.	Brief summary of next steps/ timescales, etc.	Do we have evidence that we have advised the client/sought their instructions/advised them where their file will be transferred/ monies we hold on client account, etc.? Add date of notification and details of how client was contacted.	Do we have evidence that we have client's authority to transfer their files to either a firm of our choice or their choice?

Annex 7E
Former client checklist

Former client/File reference	File audit	Has former client been notified of firm closure?	Has client responded?
Brief description of client/matter type/when file closed/what was agreed with client about storage and destruction.	Can any of the file content be returned to client/destroyed/scanned, etc.? Are we holding original documents?	Do we have evidence that we have advised the former client/sought their instructions about their files, etc.? Add date of notification and details of how former client was contacted.	Do we have evidence to show that former client is aware of location of their files/original documents?

Annex 7F
Draft letter of notification to clients

We write to inform you that the partners/directors/members of this firm have agreed to close this firm with effect from [*date*].

The firm has been sold to/is merging with [*firm name*] which practises from [*address*].

Your file will be transferred to [*firm name*] on [*date*] unless we receive your instructions to transfer your file to another firm.

For your information, we currently hold [*list any files/original documents*], as well as [£X], in our client account.

Your papers will remain in safekeeping at this address, and your money will remain on our client account until we receive your instructions, or until [*date*].

If we have not heard from you by then, [*firm name*] will assume responsibility for your papers, and hold your money on their client account, until they hear from you.

Yours sincerely

[*Signed*]

Annex 7G
Draft letter of notification to former clients

We write to inform you that the partners/directors/members of this firm have agreed to close this firm with effect from [*date*].

The firm has been sold to/is merging with [*firm name*] which practises from [*address*].

We are currently holding the following files and original documents on your behalf: [*list any files/original documents*].

We will continue to hold your file in safe storage and future enquiries can be directed to [*name*] at [*firm name*]/Your file will be transferred to [*firm name*] on [*date*] unless we receive your instructions to return your file to you.

Yours sincerely

[*Signed*]

Annex 7H

Draft letter of notification to other relevant parties

We write to inform you that the partners/directors/members have agreed to close this firm with effect from [*date*].

The firm has been sold to/is merging with [*firm name*] which practises from [*address*]. All future correspondence should be addressed to [*name*].

Please can you acknowledge safe receipt and update your records.

Yours sincerely

[*Signed*]

8 Moving to another regulator or ceasing to be a regulated practice

8.1 Who should read this chapter?

This chapter should be read by anyone continuing to provide legal services but moving to either an unregulated business or a law practice regulated by one of the other approved regulators under the Legal Services Act 2007.

8.2 Regulatory requirements

Most of this toolkit so far has focused on your regulatory obligations if you are closing your firm. However, you will also find this information helpful if you are converting to being regulated by another approved regulator, such as the Council for Licensed Conveyancers. You should therefore apply the guidance the same way.

Similarly, most of the requirements discussed so far apply to firms that will continue to provide general legal services (i.e. excluding any of the reserved legal activities) in the unregulated sector. However, at the time of writing this issue is the subject of a consultation by the SRA.

Currently, solicitors employed by an unregulated entity are restricted in whom they can advise – broadly speaking, they are restricted to just advising their employers and a limited category of third parties (see rules 1 and 4 of the SRA Practice Framework Rules 2011).

However, under the proposed SRA Handbook 2018 there will not be the same restriction. Instead, the draft Rules provide that solicitors employed in unregulated entities will nevertheless be able to provide their services as practising solicitors to clients of those entities.

9 Professional indemnity insurance: regulatory requirements

9.1 Who should read this chapter?

This chapter is essential reading for everyone who is dealing with an exit event. This is because it is a requirement of practice:

- that all firms must have a current and valid policy of professional indemnity insurance; and
- that there is appropriate coverage to continue to protect clients of a firm which ceases to exist in its current form, either because of a merger or closure.

9.2 Indemnity requirements while in practice

The following SRA Code of Conduct 2011 outcomes are relevant to this issue:

- **Outcome 1.8**: clients [must] have the benefit of your compulsory professional indemnity insurance and you do not exclude or attempt to exclude liability below the minimum level of cover required by the SRA Indemnity Insurance Rules.
- **Outcome 1.16**: you [must] inform current clients if you discover any act or omission which could give rise to a claim by them against you.
- **Outcome 7.13**: you [must] assess and purchase the level of professional indemnity insurance cover that is appropriate for your current and past practice, taking into account potential levels of claim by your clients and others and any alternative arrangements you or your client may make.

Indemnity requirements are contained in the SRA Indemnity Insurance Rules 2013. All firms carrying on a practice during any indemnity period must take out and maintain qualifying insurance provided by a participating insurer. Qualifying insurance means a policy that provides professional indemnity insurance cover in accordance with the SRA minimum terms and conditions of professional indemnity insurance (MTC).

It should be noted that the definition of 'private practice' for the purposes of the Indemnity Insurance Rules does *not* include practice consisting only of providing professional services without remuneration for friends or relatives, or to companies wholly owned by the family of the solicitor or REL, or registered charities.

A list of participating insurers is available from the SRA website (at **www.sra.org. uk/Solicitors/Code-of-Conduct/professional-indemnity/qualifying-insurers.page**).

The Indemnity Insurance Rules stipulate that recognised bodies and licensed bodies (firms that are limited companies and alternative business structures) must have at least £3 million compulsory cover for any one claim. Other types of law firms (sole practitioners and unincorporated partnerships) must have at least £2 million cover.

You should also consider whether it is appropriate to purchase top-up insurance; this does not need to be qualifying insurance.

At the time of writing the SRA is consulting on significant changes to its indemnity insurance requirements. Further information on this can be obtained from the SRA (**www.sra.org.uk**).

9.3 If a firm is unable to obtain qualifying insurance

Qualifying insurance must be in place throughout the existence of the firm.

If a firm, on or before the expiry of a policy period, fails to obtain a policy of qualifying insurance from a participating insurer commencing on the day following expiry, the firm's participating insurer is required to extend cover under the existing policy for a further 30 days.

This is known as the extended indemnity period (EIP). Firms can continue to practise as normal during this period but must notify the SRA of their circumstances as soon as reasonably practicable, and in any event no later than five days after entering the EIP.

If a firm fails to obtain an alternative policy of qualifying insurance during or before the expiry of the 30-day EIP, it must cease to practise within a further period of 60 days, unless the firm obtains a policy of qualifying insurance on or before the expiry of the 60 days which provides cover that begins or is backdated to begin with effect on and from the expiry of the policy period. This is known as the cessation period (CP).

The CP is used for the orderly closure or merger of the practice. During the CP, the firm (and its managers, employees, consultants and agents) may only engage in activities in connection with private legal practice on behalf of the firm to discharge its obligations within the scope of the existing instructions the firm held before the CP commenced, or which are necessary in connection with the discharge of such obligations.

Disciplinary action will be taken against anyone who accepts new instructions and/ or engages in other non-permitted legal activities during the CP. The firm's participating insurer is required to provide cover during the CP which, as a minimum, satisfies the MTC.

The firm must notify the SRA as soon as reasonably practicable that it is in the CP, and in any event no later than five days after entering the CP.

The SRA will work with the firm to ensure that it has ceased practice before the expiry of the 60-day CP. Firms must be aware that the participating insurer under the existing policy is not required to provide any cover beyond this period except for run-off cover for a period of six years, commencing on the expiry of the firm's final policy of qualifying insurance (excluding any extended indemnity period and CP (as may be applicable)).

9.4 Closure of the firm: ongoing indemnity considerations

Insurance cover is effected on a claims-made basis. This means that a closed firm must have run-off cover in place to deal with claims that arise in the future and in respect of the time in practice. The form that this takes is determined by whether the firm ceases to practise with or without a successor practice, and on the basis of the terms of the contract agreed with the successor practice.

The notion of successor practice is by reference to a defined term in the SRA Handbook Glossary. When discussing a purchase/merger/transfer of business with another firm, it is prudent for both parties to the negotiations to be mindful of the definition, as this has a bearing on the ongoing indemnity position of the closing firm. Both parties are advised to take legal advice as to whether the future relationship is to be regarded as a successor practice.

The definition of, and formulae for determining, a successor practice is as follows:

successor practice

(i)   means a practice identified in this definition as 'B', where:

(A) 'A' is the practice to which B succeeds; and
(B) 'A's owner' is the owner of A immediately prior to transition; and
(C) 'B's owner' is the owner of B immediately following transition; and
(D) 'transition' means merger, acquisition, absorption or other transition which results in A no longer being carried on as a discrete legal practice.

(ii) B is a successor practice to A where:

(A) B is or was held out, expressly or by implication, by B's owner as being the successor of A or as incorporating A, whether such holding out is contained in notepaper, business cards, form of electronic communications, publications, promotional material or otherwise, or is contained in any statement or declaration by B's owner to any regulatory or taxation authority; and/or

(B) (where A's owner was a sole practitioner and the transition occurred on or before 31 August 2000) – the sole practitioner is a principal of B's owner; and/or

(C) (where A's owner was a sole practitioner and the transition occurred on or after 1 September 2000) – the sole practitioner is a principal or employee of B's owner; and/or

(D) (where A's owner was a recognised body or a licensed body (in respect of its regulated activities)) – that body is a principal of B's owner; and/or

(E) (where A's owner was a partnership) – the majority of the principals of A's owner have become principals of B's owner; and/or

(F) (where A's owner was a partnership and the majority of principals of A's owner did not become principals of the owner of another legal practice as a result of the transition) – one or more of the principals of A's owner have become principals of B's owner and:

    (I) B is carried on under the same name as A or a name which substantially incorporates the name of A (or a substantial part of the name of A); and/or

    (II) B is carried on from the same premises as A; and/or

    (III) the owner of B acquired the goodwill and/or assets of A; and/or

    (IV) the owner of B assumed the liabilities of A; and/or

    (V) the majority of staff employed by A's owner became employees of B's owner.

(iii) Notwithstanding the foregoing, B is not a successor practice to A under paragraph (ii) (B), (C), (D), (E) or (F) if another practice is or was held out by the owner of that other practice as the successor of A or as incorporating A, provided that there is insurance complying with the MTC in relation to that other practice.

This definition and formula is complicated and sometimes difficult to interpret. The trigger event for determining whether there is a successor practice situation is an understanding of the meaning of 'transition'.

Transition is defined as meaning a merger, acquisition, absorption or other transition taken place which results in a firm no longer being carried on as a discrete legal *practice*. This event occurs through a number of alternative sets of circumstances, any one of which is sufficient to evidence transition and the creation of a successor practice.

The following box gives examples of transition events. This is a description of an imaginary firm, First & Co, which is closing down and in discussions with another firm, Second Solicitors. Is Second Solicitors a successor practice?

Examples of transition events that create a successor practice

- Second Solicitors holds itself out to the SRA or HMRC as the successor practice to First & Co.
- Second Solicitors publishes information claiming to be the successor practice to First & Co.
- First & Co is a sole practitioner and he or she becomes a partner or employee of Second Solicitors, unless another *practice* is or was held out by the owner of that other *practice* as the successor of First & Co or as incorporating First & Co, provided that there is insurance complying with the MTC in relation to that other *practice*.
- First & Co is an authorised company, etc. and that firm becomes a principal of Second Solicitors, unless another *practice* is or was held out by the owner of that other *practice* as the successor of First & Co or as incorporating First & Co, provided that there is insurance complying with the MTC in relation to that other *practice*.
- First & Co is a partnership and the majority of partners become partners in Second Solicitors, unless another *practice* is or was held out by the owner of that other *practice* as the successor of First & Co or as incorporating First & Co, provided that there is insurance complying with the MTC in relation to that other *practice*.
- First & Co is a partnership, and while the majority of partners did not become principals of another legal practice, one or more of the partners in First & Co became a principal(s) in Second Solicitors and one or more of the following additional conditions is present:

    - Second Solicitors is carried on under either the same name as First & Co or substantially the same name as First & Co; and/or
    - Second Solicitors is carried on from First & Co's premises; and/or
    - Second Solicitors acquired First & Co's goodwill or assets; and/or
    - Second Solicitors assumed First & Co's liabilities; and/or
    - the majority of First & Co's staff became employees of Second Solicitors, unless another *practice* is or was held out by the owner of that other *practice* as the successor of First & Co or as incorporating First & Co, provided that there is insurance complying with the MTC in relation to that other *practice*.

It is the last scenario (i.e. the circumstance in (ii)(F) of the defined term) which is the least clear-cut of all the possible outcomes connected with a transition event.

Both the SRA and your insurer will be able to assist with any further clarification you may need.

9.5 Indemnity considerations on the closure of your practice and no successor practice

If your firm closes and there is not a successor practice (as defined), then the closing firm's participating insurer on the date of closure must provide six years' run-off cover. The premium charged for this compulsory cover will be included in the policy terms. Excesses will usually continue to apply during this period.

9.6 Indemnity considerations on the closure of your practice if there is a successor practice

If there is a successor practice, then there are two options:

- Run-off cover for the ceased practice may be provided through the successor practice's insurance, meaning that there is no need to trigger the run-off mechanisms in your own insurance.

  Excess payments, and liability for payment of these, will be a contractual consideration with the successor practice. In the event that you remain liable, it is sensible to agree that the successor practice will provide you with ongoing details of their future arrangements and excesses agreed.
- Despite the existence of a successor practice, you may elect to have run-off cover with your own insurer, in which event this insurer must be notified of your decision and you must continue to pay the run-off premiums.

9.7 What happens at the end of the run-off period?

At the end of the period, post six years run-off will start. The terms of this cover will be the same as that provided by the participating insurer but at no extra cost to you or the successor practice.

Currently, the Board of the Solicitors Indemnity Fund Ltd, with the endorsement of the Law Society, has put in place an insurance programme for the period up to 30 September 2020. Arrangements for the position beyond this date will be disclosed in due course.

9.8 Further resources and help

- Law Society's Professional Indemnity Insurance Practice Note (see **www.lawsociety.org.uk/support-services/advice/practice-notes/professional-indemnity-insurance**).
- Law Society professional indemnity insurance retirement calculator (see **www.lawsociety.org.uk/support-services/risk-compliance/pii**).

- Law Society online articles:

  - 'Extended indemnity period' (published 9 October 2014, see **www.lawsociety. org.uk/support-services/advice/articles/extended-indemnity-period**).
  - 'Professional indemnity insurance – 10 key questions answered' (published 24 July 2017, see **www.lawsociety.org.uk/support-services/advice/articles/ professional-indemnity-insurance-10-key-questions-answered**).

- SRA guidance 'Professional indemnity insurance' (last updated 11 July 2016, see **www.sra.org.uk/solicitors/code-of-conduct/indemnity.page**).
- SRA support resources for small firms (see **www.sra.org.uk/solicitors/supervision/ small-firms-help.page**).

Annex 9A
Indemnity decisions flowchart

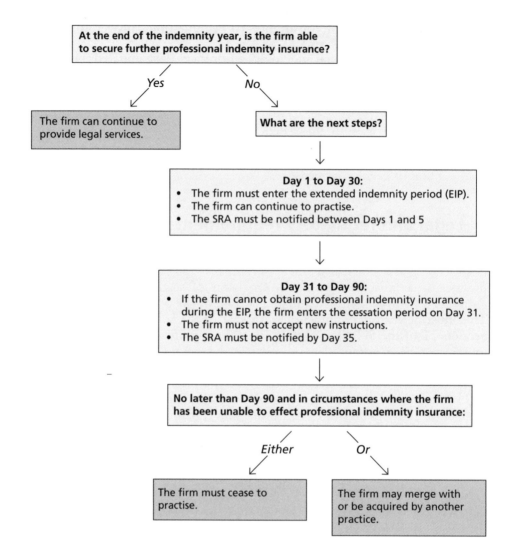

10 Life after an exit event: options and regulatory considerations

10.1 Who should read this chapter?

Everyone who exits a firm, for whatever reason, must be confident that they understand how they can hold themselves out, and what activities they can perform after the exit event. Making the wrong decision may result in the commission of a criminal act and/or regulatory censure.

10.2 Legal and regulatory requirements

- **Section 1A of the Solicitors Act 1974** (as amended): you are regarded in law to be practising as a solicitor if you are on the roll and you are employed in private practice in connection with the provision of legal services in both SRA-authorised firms and firms regulated by one of the other authorised regulators. This must be read in conjunction with s.21 of the Solicitors Act 1974.
- **Section 21 of the Solicitors Act 1974**: to be qualified to act as a solicitor, you must have been admitted as a solicitor, be on the roll and have a current practising certificate. This means that you will be committing a criminal offence under s.21, as well as being in breach of the SRA Practice Framework Rules 2011, if you use any description which implies that you are qualified to act as a solicitor and you do not have a practising certificate.

As specified in the SRA Handbook 2011, Version 19:

- **Rule 9, SRA Practice Framework Rules 2011:** If you are practising as a solicitor (including in-house), whether in England and Wales or overseas, you must:
  (a) have in force a practising certificate issued by the SRA; or
  (b) be exempt under section 88 of the Solicitors Act from holding a practising certificate.

  You will be practising as a solicitor if you are involved in legal practice and:
  (a) your involvement in the firm or the work depends on your being a solicitor;
  (b) you are held out explicitly or implicitly as a practising solicitor;
  (c) you are employed explicitly or implicitly as a solicitor; or
  (d) you are deemed by section 1A of the Solicitors Act to be acting as a solicitor.

  'Legal practice' includes not only the provision of legal advice or assistance, or representation in connection with the application of the law or resolution of legal disputes, but also the provision of other services such as are provided by solicitors.

If you are a solicitor who was formerly an REL, and you are practising from an office in the UK as a lawyer of an Establishment Directive profession, you must have in force a practising certificate issued by the SRA, even if you are not practising as a solicitor.

Other SRA Handbook requirements:

- In addition, solicitors who are not practising, but choose to remain on the roll of solicitors, must continue to comply with the following Principles:
    - **Principle 1:** you must uphold the rule of law and the proper administration of justice.
    - **Principle 2:** you must act with integrity.
    - **Principle 6:** you must behave in a way that maintains the trust the public places in you and in the provision of legal services.

10.3 Can you be described as a solicitor if you do not hold a practising certificate?

If you remain on the roll, but choose not to have a current practising certificate, you can describe yourself as a solicitor but only in situations where there is no implication that you are practising as a solicitor.

Such an implication could arise if you are a director or office holder in an organisation that gives legal advice as part of its activities. In such circumstances – and regardless of whether you are personally involved in this aspect of the business – it is advisable to make your status clear by ensuring that any description or reference to you as a solicitor is qualified by words such as 'non-practising'.

10.4 Can you return to work in private practice but not as a solicitor?

If the cause of your exit is a disciplinary issue that has led to an order suspending you from practice or prohibiting you from working in an SRA-authorised firm, or similar, then this disciplinary event is a key determining factor when considering future possibilities. You must consider and avoid any future employment that places you in breach of the disciplinary sanction.

In other circumstances, if you remain on the roll, you must hold a practising certificate if you are employed in connection with the provision of legal services in an SRA-authorised entity. This need to hold a practising certificate originates in s.1A of the Solicitors Act 1974, and is reinforced by regulatory requirements in rule 9 of the SRA Practice Framework Rules 2011, as described at **10.2**.

In more detail, s.1A is drafted, and interpreted, so that you will be held in law to be practising as a solicitor in a number of circumstances. For example, you must comply with s.1A even if:

- you are not held out as a solicitor;
- you are only doing unreserved legal activities;
- you are working without remuneration;
- you are employed on only a temporary or occasional basis.

This broad statutory position means that simply avoiding the use of the title 'solicitor' is not sufficient to avoid the requirement to have a current practising certificate.

A number of law firm roles will trigger the need for a practising certificate if the role-holder is on the roll. For example:

- paralegal;
- book-keeper dealing with duties relating to the SRA Accounts Rules;
- professional support services or knowledge management role;
- compliance officer for legal practice;
- compliance professional;
- conflicts analyst;
- secretarial support to fee earners.

To avoid a breach of the Solicitors Act 1974, and the regulatory requirements of the SRA Practice Framework Rules 2011, you must either hold a current practising certificate or apply to come off the roll.

If your preferred option is to remove your name from the roll, you must ensure that you are not held out in a way which suggests that you are entitled to practise as a solicitor.

You will also need to avoid using titles or descriptions that would hold you out – either explicitly or implicitly – as a practising lawyer. This includes the word 'lawyer' itself, plus titles such as 'counsel' or 'attorney', unless you hold another qualification and you are practising in that capacity only.

If you do not hold a current practising certificate, you should avoid the following job titles:

- lawyer;
- counsel;
- attorney;
- legal adviser;
- legal associate;
- legal consultant;
- legal executive;
- legal expert;
- legal specialist;
- legal practitioner;
- legal officer.

In addition, you need to ensure that you no longer conduct reserved legal activities (as described in s.12 of the Legal Services Act 2007) in your own right, although you are able to perform reserved legal activities under the supervision of a person who is authorised to do these activities.

The list below details the different types of reserved legal activities; these are reserved by statute to practising solicitors and certain other qualified persons. It is a criminal offence to perform any of these activities for a fee, gain or reward unless this is as a qualified person or under the supervision of a qualified person.

The reserved legal activities are:

- exercising a right of audience;
- the conduct of litigation;
- reserved instrument activities;
- probate activities;
- notarial activities; and
- the administration of oaths.

10.5 Can you work in an in-house role as a solicitor?

'In-house' is the term used to describe the position of solicitors who are employed in non SRA-authorised businesses.

It is not uncommon for a solicitor exiting private practice to move into an in-house role. Often this will be a move to a previous client's business to provide the same or similar services, but as an employee rather than an external adviser.

There are a number of legal and regulatory considerations to bear in mind:

- Has there been a disciplinary finding and sanction that prohibits this form of employment?
- What are you being asked to do? Bear in mind the restrictions on in-house employment currently contained in the SRA Practice Framework Rules 2011. If you are being employed to provide legal services, then you must understand rules 1 and 4 of the Practice Framework Rules:
  - **Rule 1** allows an in-house solicitor to provide legal services to your employer.
  - **Rule 4** extends this starting point but in a very limited form so that, for example, you can act for group companies but only if this does not create a conflict with your employer client. In other words, this is a regulatory position which restricts your right to provide legal services in ways which would be different to private practice.

- Are you being employed as a solicitor? If this is the case, you need to hold a practising certificate unless you can rely on the statutory exemption in s.88 of the Solicitors Act 1974. Section 88 exempts certain solicitors to public bodies from holding a practising certificate.

- Are you employed as a practising solicitor?
- Are you held out as being a solicitor?
- Are you doing reserved legal activities or supervising others performing such activities?

10.6 Can you remain on a firm's notepaper as a consultant?

This question may arise in circumstances where you retire from a continuing business. If you are completely retired but choose to remain on the roll, you can be included on the firm's notepaper and other forms of publicity as a consultant, but only if the fact that you are not practising is made clear by use of additional wording such as 'non-practising' or 'retired'. In these circumstances, you must avoid undertaking any legal work at all.

10.7 Can you provide legal services to friends and relatives?

As a non-practising solicitor you cannot undertake reserved legal activities for anyone, including friends and family, unless one of the following circumstances is relevant:

- you are able to rely on authorisation in some capacity other than as a solicitor; or
- in relation to reserved instrument and probate activities, the work is not being done for, or in expectation of, any fee, gain or reward.

As a non-practising solicitor, you may do other legal work (i.e. work that is not a reserved legal activity) for friends and relatives. You must explain that you are not doing the work as a solicitor and that you are not covered by professional indemnity insurance.

10.8 Can you witness/certify documents?

This is determined by whether the document must be witnessed/certified by a practising solicitor, in which case this may be undertaken only by an individual holding a current practising certificate.

Where this is not a pre-condition, it is advisable to make your status clear by describing yourself as a retired or non-practising solicitor.

10.9 Can you continue to act as an executor or trustee?

If you continue to act as a professional executor or trustee after retirement, you are regarded as being in practice, meaning that you must satisfy the following conditions:

- You must apply to the SRA to be recognised as a sole practitioner unless you are exempt under rule 10.2 of the SRA Practice Framework Rules.
- You must comply with the SRA Indemnity Insurance Rules unless your practice is exempt (see **9.2**).
- You must comply with the SRA Accounts Rules unless you are able to claim exemption under rule 32.1A.
- You must hold a practising certificate.

Alternatively, you may decide to continue acting in a private capacity rather than as a solicitor. This means:

- You must not charge for any work.
- You must not describe yourself as a solicitor unless this is qualified by 'non-practising'.
- You must advise third parties (banks, beneficiaries, etc.) of your change of status.
- You must explain the implications of your change of status to co-trustees and to the beneficiaries in terms of your ability to charge, and the professional indemnity position.

APPENDIX A

Closing Down Your Practice: Regulatory Requirements Practice Note

Last updated: 25 August 2017

1   Introduction

1.1 Who should read this practice note?

All solicitors who are involved in the management of their practice – and in particular the Compliance Officer for Legal Practice (COLP) – should have a plan in place for closure.

This practice note will be of particular interest to any solicitor who is contemplating closing down their practice (e.g. due to retirement) and contains information regarding the regulatory requirements.

However all solicitors would benefit from being aware of the requirements in this document.

1.2 What is the issue?

This practice note outlines the regulatory requirements relating to closing down a practice. There are numerous actions and costs involved in closing down a firm which require forward planning. The process for closing a practice differs depending on whether or not there is a successor practice in place. For further information about the successor practice rules, consult the Professional Indemnity Insurance (PII) practice note.

Solicitors should be aware of the effects that these pressures can have on their psychological and emotional wellbeing as well as that of their staff, and should seek assistance where necessary (please see the end of this note for further guidance). They must also plan ahead if they are to ensure they minimise any potential problems with closure.

2   Planning to close down your practice

Outcome 7.2 of the SRA Code requires that 'you have effective systems and controls in place to achieve and comply with all the Principles, rules and outcomes and other requirements of the Handbook, where applicable'.

Outcome 7.3 requires that you ' identify, monitor and manage risks to compliance with all the Principles, rules and outcomes and other requirements of the Handbook, if applicable to you, and take steps to address issues identified'.

It should be part of your firm's risk management procedures to have a plan in place for an orderly close-down and to deal with outstanding issues such as client matters, client money, insurance and other administrative functions.

This may be particularly important for sole practitioners, where disciplinary action or long-term incapacity could force the closure of the practice.

In your plan for firm closure, you may wish to consider:

*   how clients will be informed of the closure;
*   not taking on new work that could continue beyond the intended closure date (such as litigation, complicated matrimonial or probate cases, or conveyancing);
*   who else needs to be notified of the closure;
*   how active matters will be transferred to a successor firm/another firm;
*   dealing with client files (archiving closed files is one of the highest costs of closure);
*   returning money on account to clients;
*   run-off professional indemnity insurance cover and how this will be paid for (usually two to three times the firm's annual premium);
*   if this will result in staff being made redundant, you should ensure that you are compliant with relevant employment law (such as ensuring you appropriately consult with your employees) and that you make financial provision for the payment of statutory redundancy pay and – where appropriate – the issue of pay in lieu of notice. (Please see section 4.5 for further information.)

As well as being aware of regulatory requirements, it is also important to bear in mind that there are a range of non-regulatory issues which you may wish to consider. For example:

*   whether you wish to purchase run-off cover for longer than the mandatory six year period (see 4.4 below);
*   the financial impacts of winding down your workload.

3   Reasons for closing down or selling your practice

3.1 Disciplinary action or bankruptcy

There are cases where disciplinary action or bankruptcy, leading to suspension of a practising certificate, can force firms to close. This would clearly be the case for sole practitioners as loss of a practising certificate means they are no longer entitled to be recognised sole practitioners. The SRA has powers to withdraw authorisation from firms, preventing them from offering reserved legal services to the public.

Disciplinary action and bankruptcy are often foreseeable events and you should, where possible, make contingency arrangements to close or sell the practice before these events occur. Failure to do so is likely to lead to an intervention which will be costly to you and disruptive to clients and those involved with the firm. You must take into account the outcomes in chapter 7 of the Handbook on 'Management of your business'.

3.2 Failure to secure PII

Firms have a continuing obligation to ensure they have qualifying insurance in place at all times or face closure. Firms have 30 days from expiry of the last policy (Extended Indemnity Period) to secure cover, followed by a 60-day Cessation Period to close down, during which they cannot take on new work.

In this situation, the SRA can extract undertakings from firms to organise their closure in a very short timeframe. If they fail to do so, the firm can be accused of not managing an effective close-down and can be sanctioned for failing to comply with an undertaking. It is therefore imperative that the firm has a plan in place for closing down.

3.3 Illness, death and other emergencies

Health issues may affect the ability to practise. These can affect solicitors at any stage of their career.

While there is no explicit requirement to plan for the possibility of illness or death in the SRA Code, chapter 7 includes the following Indicative Behaviour:

> IB (7.4) making arrangements for the continuation of your firm in the event of absences and emergencies, for example holiday or sick leave, with the minimum interruption to clients' business.

Sole practitioners should nominate someone to deal with their practice in the event of their death/incapacity. You will naturally want to avoid a situation in which the SRA will intervene and the associated costs are borne by your estate.

You should also consider seeking advice from your insurance broker about whether there are any additional insurance products available to assist in these circumstances.

The following section gives more details on these matters, if required.

3.3.1   SRA Handbook advice

Please refer to the SRA Handbook for guidance on the following:

- Information requirements to notify changes, including due to illness (Rules 8.7–8.8);
- Death (Rule 23.3); and
- Ceasing to be approved (Rule 23.4).

3.3.2 Suggestions for sole practitioners

At a local level, sole practitioners may want to pair up in a kind of buddy system, whereby if one dies or is otherwise incapable of managing his or her affairs, then the other agrees to step in and manage the closure of the dead or incapacitated solicitor's firm. Alternatively, sole practitioners may want to make arrangements for the appointment of a practitioner locum to carry out this work.

3.3.3 Involvement of non-solicitors

It would also be possible for non-solicitor family members to wind up the firm in the case of death or emergency, but there are strict rules regarding how. We would encourage members to be aware of this issue and to inform those who have been nominated or who are likely to step in under such circumstances of the processes and issues involved, as well as any contingency plans they have prepared. It is advisable to have a written closure plan setting out relevant information and contact details (particularly for sole practitioners). A copy of this should be readily accessible to those likely to have to deal with the practice in case of death or emergency. It is likely that the personal representatives will not have access to the same resources as a practising solicitor, so it is essential to leave a sufficiently detailed and clear plan (e.g. including a link to this note), as well as advising non-solicitors of the need for client confidentiality. In the case of deceased sole practitioners, there is a special process available (the SRA temporary authorisation process), which would allow his or her executor, or an office manager appointed by the deceased practitioner's personal representative, or an appropriate employee to have temporary authorisation. There is a form to apply for this (FA7), which is available on request from the SRA. You can enquire about [at this email address: **authorisation@sra.org.uk**].

It is important to note that help and guidance are available for solicitors and non-solicitors who find themselves in some of the difficult situations above, or who find themselves supporting those who are. The organisations named in part 5 of this note would be able to offer further advice and support to those in need of information or further guidance.

3.3.4 Other reasons

There are of course many other reasons why someone may want or need to close down their practice. For example, solicitors may choose to do so in order to study, pursue a different career, or for family reasons (e.g. long-term maternity leave).

Some solicitors may also decide to close their firm to enter the judiciary. More information about becoming a judge is available [at **www.lawsociety.org.uk/law-careers/solicitor-judges-division**].

4   Closing down your practice

You must close down your firm in an orderly and transparent fashion (chapter 10 of the SRA Code, outcome 10.13). It is recommended that your firm sets out and follows a closure plan relevant to its circumstances so as to achieve an orderly wind-down of its work.

Failure to close down the practice in an appropriate way that puts client protection or the reputation of the profession at risk, can lead to:

* disciplinary action;
* an intervention, which is likely to prove costly to you, both financially and reputationally;
* where clients have received poor service, an ombudsman's decision against you.

As a solicitor, it is also important that you inform the relevant authorities and deal with all relevant outstanding client matters. It is equally important that you do not continue to provide reserved legal services to clients once your firm ceases or is sold (unless it is through another regulated entity).

These may include the SRA, HMRC, your accountants, your bank or building society, companies or LLPs using your office as a registered address, your Counsel's chambers, court offices and court records, the Crown Prosecution Service and police, directories (professional, telephone, business, etc.), the Information Commissioner (data protection), any introducers with whom you have an arrangement, the Land Charges Registry (key number), the Land Registry, your landlord, the Legal Aid Agency, your local authority (regarding business rates), the London Gazette and one other newspaper (not necessary for mergers), and any mortgage lenders where you are on the panel.

4.1 Clients

4.1.1   Introduction

You must inform clients if you are closing your practice. You should try to give your clients enough notice so that they can instruct another firm, and should ensure that clients are aware that they are free to instruct any firm. If you hold client money, you will need the client's informed consent to transfer the money.

If obtaining client consent is not possible due to an urgent need to transfer files (e.g. a risk that the office will be repossessed and files removed), you may consider arranging for another SRA-regulated firm to take on any remaining clients. Transferring files to another firm before clients have given consent carries significant risks, including breach of trust, breach of confidentiality, and possibly causing a serious complaint if the new firm has a conflict, or the client would not want to instruct them. The new firm will need to contact clients urgently and seek consent properly. In order to help facilitate this process, it is recommended that firms carry out regular audits in order to identify and close down client files as part of good practice management.

You should identify any work in progress or retainers that have not been closed. After the firm has closed, you should be careful not to practise or be held out as practising through the firm when tying up loose ends for clients. If you do practise once your PII has expired, this work will not be covered by your run-off cover.

You should inform former clients who might be affected by the closure, e.g. those you hold papers for or have appointed you as an executor in your professional capacity. If you have been acting as a personal representative or trustee you must reconsider whether you can still continue to act in a professional or personal capacity. You must give due consideration to any conditional fee agreements (CFAs) at all times, with particular care required over the pre LASPO CFAs for personal injury work.

Some of these and other issues to be aware of, concerning clients, are covered below in further detail.

4.1.2   Client Confidentiality

It is a legal and regulatory requirement to ensure that client confidentiality is protected. This duty continues after the conclusion of your client's matter. You must also consider confidentiality when transferring client matters or when storing files.

The SRA has provided further guidance on confidentiality requirements in relation to mergers or acquisitions of practices.[1]

This guidance specifically warns solicitors against sharing confidential information with third parties without the informed consent of clients and points to mergers and acquisitions as situations where this may occur. It questions whether it is necessary for external people to see client files when they are assessing a firm's financial stability (key points below):

'Due diligence or an assessment of a firm's viability should be focused on the firm's financial situation, financial records, accounts, financial forecasts and forward plans. Firms must take steps to minimise the risk of third parties having access to client information ... During negotiations sufficient steps need to be taken to protect confidential client information and, where appropriate, to seek clients' consent to any disclosure of confidential information.'

4.1.3   Client Files and Data Protection

You must consider what to do with client files. See our practice notes on file closure management and file retention trusts for further information.

---

1   www.sra.org.uk/solicitors/code-of-conduct/guidance/guidance/Protecting-and-maintaining-client-confidentiality.page

You should remember that some of the papers in the file belong to the client and therefore you may not be able to destroy them. If your firm is being sold, the new owner may agree to store the files. If you are closing down you should, where possible, return them to the client. Where the client is untraceable, you may in some cases be able to destroy the file if you have reserved the right to do so. In other cases, you may need to arrange suitable storage.

You must inform the SRA about the location of the files.

You should also be aware of the requirements for enhanced measures to protect personal data which will apply when the General Data Protection Regulation (GDPR) comes into force in May 2018. The requirements for consent to disclosure are much stricter and measures designed to prevent Data Protection Act breaches will need to be embedded in internal procedures, so there should be provision for this in any closure plan. A webinar on GDPR preparedness is available.

4.1.4   Client accounts

If you are closing down you should where possible transfer all client money out of client accounts by:

- paying disbursements;
- billing for outstanding costs;
- accounting to clients;
- transferring client monies to a new firm where the client has requested or consented to the transfer.

Money that remains after the closure must be dealt with in accordance with the SRA Accounts Rules. The practice note on residual client balances sets out what you will need to do if clients are untraceable.

Since October 2014, residual client balances of £500 or less can now be dealt with by firms without authorisation from the SRA. It is important to note that if your practice is being sold, the new owner must set up new client accounts that are distinguishable from the ones held by you.

4.1.5   Selling your practice

You must inform clients of the change in ownership before it occurs to ensure you comply with the following principles of the SRA Code:

- acting in your clients' best interests (principle 4);
- providing them with a proper standard of service (principle 5).

You should provide clients with information to allow them to make an informed choice about whether they continue to instruct the 'new firm' (i.e. the firm once it has changed ownership).

If the new firm will be SRA regulated, you can seek your clients' instructions as to whether they want to transfer to the new firm. If you wish, you can set a deadline for clients to respond, after which you may transfer the file to the new firm. New firms must be authorised.

Although pre-authorisation can be applied for in the event of a planned closure, if there is likely to be a gap before the new firm is authorised you must inform clients of their options (e.g. instructing an alternative solicitor).

If the new firm will not be SRA regulated, you must explain who the regulator will be, what their status is, the implications for client protections and duties owed to clients. You must have explicit consent to transfer clients' files and money to the new firm. If clients do not consent, you may need to continue to hold on to their files and monies within the client account. Clients should be made aware that you will not be able to continue to work on their matters without that consent.

If you are closing down with your firm under a partial successor agreement, you need to notify your clients and explain exactly what this means. To take one example, you may wish to note that a new owner may only be taking on the goodwill of your firm, but not any existing client files which will remain covered under your PII, and not that of the new firm.

4.2 Informing the SRA

You must inform the SRA of your intention for the firm to cease practising and consider the outcomes in chapter 10 on 'You and your regulator' of the SRA Code, particularly outcome (10.13):

> **Outcome (10.13)** Once you are aware that your firm will cease to practise, you effect the orderly and transparent wind-down of activities, including informing the SRA before the firm closes.

You can inform the SRA by contacting your firm's SRA supervisor, or by email, marked for the attention of the regulatory notifications team. The notification should include:

- the date on which the firm will cease to practice;
- the reason for closure;
- a request to revoke your firm's authorisation or your recognition as a sole practitioner from the date of closure;
- where remaining client files and documents will be stored;
- the name of the firm, practising address and any trading names you use.

You should also notify the SRA when all matters have been dealt with and the firm is fully closed.

Any firm that is regulated by the SRA and is buying your firm must inform the SRA as this is likely to be considered a material change to relevant information about the firm. You must also inform the SRA of any material changes to relevant information about you. This includes you moving to a new firm. This is outlined in chapter 10 of the SRA Code:

> Outcome (10.3) You notify the SRA promptly of any material changes to relevant information about you including serious financial difficulty, action taken against you by another regulator and serious failure to comply with or achieve the Principles, rules, outcomes and other requirements of the Handbook.

4.3 Compliance officers

The SRA Authorisation Rules outline the requirements for the roles of compliance officer for legal practice (COLP) and compliance officer for finance and administration (COFA). See our practice note on compliance officers for more detailed information about these roles.

You should consider contingency planning if, for whatever reason, a compliance officer cannot fulfil their role and you or your firm have to manage in their absence. The COLP and COFA will be instrumental in the planning of, and actions required to, close down the practice. If your practice ceases to have a compliance officer, you will need to do the following (either immediately or within seven days):

- inform the SRA;
- designate another manager or employee to replace its previous compliance officer; and
- make an application to the SRA for temporary emergency approval of a compliance officer, as appropriate (rule 18 of the SRA Authorisation Rules) followed by a permanent application if appropriate.

4.4 Professional indemnity insurers

You must discuss your plan to close with your indemnity insurer. You must inform your insurer if you have been suspended, struck off or there has been an insolvency event. If there is no successor practice, you must purchase run-off cover for six years from the date that your current policy would have expired. The cost of run-off cover is set out in your PII policy.

For further advice please refer to the Law Society's advice on run-off cover. If you have failed to renew your PII, you must inform your insurer on cover at the time your firm ceases within five business days. There is no longer an assigned risks pool for firms unable to obtain insurance on the open market. Instead, firms will enter into an extended indemnity period (of 90 days) and cessation period covered by the last insurer. The Law Society has also published advice on the extended indemnity period.

Firms have the first 30 days of the 90-day period to find insurance and 60 days, the cessation period, to organise orderly closure if unsuccessful. You must also notify the SRA within five business days that you have entered the extended indemnity period (i.e. the first 30 days of the extended indemnity period), and also if you have entered the cessation period (i.e. the final 60 days of the extended indemnity period), by email. During the 60-day cessation period, you are not permitted to take on new work but are permitted to continue to work for existing clients while closing your business in an orderly manner.

You can continue to try to secure PII cover to avoid closure before the 60 days' cessation period ends. If there is a successor practice, claims made after the closure of the practice will be dealt with by the new practice's qualifying insurer unless you have elected to secure run-off cover for the prior practice prior to succession.

A successor practice is defined in the minimum terms and conditions (MTC) in the SRA Indemnity Insurance Rules. For further information see the Law Society's PII practice note. The SRA can provide further guidance on this issue and can be contacted by email or by calling 0370 606 2555.

4.4.1   Cost of run-off

If you are considering closing your practice, you should consider the PII implications, particularly the cost of run-off cover.

The cost of MTC run-off is linked to a firm's annual premium and is typically between two or three times a firm's annual premium. You can calculate costs with the Law Society's PII retirement calculator [**www.lawsociety.org.uk/advice/articles/pii-retirement-calculator**].

4.4.2   Run-off at the end of the cessation period

If the firm closes on or before the expiry of the cessation period, the firm must be provided run-off cover by its insurer for six years incepting with effect on and from the start of the extended indemnity period.

More information about run-off cover [is available at **www.lawsociety.org.uk/Advice/Articles/Run-off-cover**].

4.4.3   Post six-year run-off cover

Your insurer is only required to provide run-off cover for six years. Claims made after this run-off period will not be covered by your PII under the SRA's MTCs.

The Solicitors Indemnity Fund (SIF) currently provides all firms with post six-year run-off cover, but it is closing in 2020. From 2020 onwards SIF will no longer provide cover for firms that closed after 31 August 2000.

Unless you put in place post six-year run-off cover insurance, to cover the period after 2020, partners of firms that close without a successor practice may be held personally liable for historical claims.

4.5 Informing staff

You will need to consider issues such as redundancy, references and ensuring that there are sufficient staff to assist you in effecting an orderly closure. If you are making 20 or more staff redundant from one establishment in a 90-day period you must follow legal requirements on 'collective consultation',[2] which can be a costly and time-consuming process if you get it wrong. There are also pension issues that could affect your practice's staff to be aware of.

You may also wish to plan staffing levels and costs ahead for the period until you close. This is because it may be expensive to temporarily replace staff who decide to leave a firm once they know it is closing.

For further details please refer to the government's redundancy consultation website or ACAS's website.

4.6 Informing other parties

You should inform the bank of your plans and also if you have been struck off or suspended.

You may also need to contact some or all of the organisations listed below to inform them of the closure of your practice:

- Accountants
- Anyone using your office as a registered address
- Counsel's chambers
- Court offices
- Crown Prosecution Service/police
- Directories – professional/telephone
- HMRC
- Information Commissioner (data protection)
- Introducers with whom you have an arrangement
- Landlord
- Land Registry/Land Charges Registry (regarding current matters)
- Legal Aid Agency
- Local authority
- London Gazette/newspaper
- Mortgage lenders where you are on the panel
- Other solicitors firms/professionals with whom you are professionally engaged
- Service providers

---

2   www.gov.uk/staff-redundant/redundancy-consultations

4.7 Notepaper, emails, etc.

Once your firm has closed, your notepaper, emails, website, etc., should reflect the fact that the firm has closed. Similarly, it should be made clear to those calling or visiting the office that the firm has now closed. If you do not hold a practising certificate, you should refer to yourself as 'non- practising'.

4.8 Undertakings

Sole practitioners or managers of firms remain responsible for any undertakings given by the firm even after it has closed. You should therefore seek to discharge any undertakings where possible. If you are unable to discharge an undertaking you may be able to transfer responsibility for carrying out the undertaking to another firm. However, you remain liable unless the recipient releases you from the undertaking.

4.9 SRA rules on records and documents

The SRA requires you to keep certain records for defined periods, for instance:

- in relation to your accounts for six years (see rule 29 of the SRA Accounts Rules);
- records made in relation to the SRA Financial Services (Conduct of Business) Rules 2001 for six years.

There may also be records that would be helpful to keep in case an issue arises at a later date, e.g. agreements relating to financial arrangements with an introducer or evidence of a client's consent to you retaining commission.

There may also be legal requirements to keep documents, e.g. VAT records.

4.10 Fraud

Solicitors' firms make attractive targets for criminals as they provide ideal vehicles to launder money and to commit fraud. The sale of a firm could be a particular target for fraudsters due to the large amounts of money that could be transferred. If you plan to sell your firm you should carry out due diligence on any potential buyer.

4.11 Financial difficulties

If the firm is in financial difficulty, you must contact the SRA. See more about reporting requirements [at **www.lawsociety.org.uk/Advice/Articles/SRA-reporting-requirements**].

If you are declared bankrupt your practising certificate will automatically be suspended and you will not be able to practise. You can apply to the SRA to have this suspension lifted. If you know you are likely to be adjudged bankrupt, you can apply in advance for the suspension to be lifted on the same day it is suspended. However, bear in mind it may well be reinstated subject to conditions. The rules of bankruptcy also mean that you will not be able to run a business.

You must inform the SRA and your insurers of the appointment of an administrative receiver, administrator or liquidator.

5   More information

...

5.6 Sane

Closing a business can potentially be a stressful and distressing process in some circumstances. If you or members of your staff require emotional or mental health support services, you can contact Sane [**www.sane.org.uk/what_we_do/support**] confidentially.

5.7 Your local Law Society

If your reasons for closing down are financial, or you are facing the possibility of being struck off or suspended, some local Law Societies may be able to assist in providing you with details of firms interested in a merger, buying your practice, or taking on existing client matters.

APPENDIX B

Further resources and information

B1　SRA rules and regulations

List of current relevant provisions in the SRA Handbook 2011

- SRA Principles 2011
- SRA Code of Conduct 2011
- SRA Accounts Rules 2011
- SRA Practice Framework Rules 2011
- SRA Authorisation Rules 2011
- SRA Practising Regulations 2011
- SRA Conduct of Business Rules 2011

Relevant extracts from the draft SRA Handbook 2018

Draft SRA Code of Conduct for Solicitors, RELs and RFLs

Maintaining trust and acting fairly

...

1.3　You perform all undertakings given by you, and do so within an agreed timescale or if no timescale has been agreed then within a reasonable amount of time.

Draft SRA Code of Conduct for Firms

Maintaining trust and acting fairly

...

1.3　You perform all undertakings given by you, and do so within an agreed timescale or if no timescale has been agreed then within a reasonable amount of time.

Compliance and business systems

2.1　You have effective governance structures, arrangements, systems and controls in place that ensure:

a)　you comply with all the SRA's regulatory arrangements, as well as with other regulatory and legislative requirements, which apply to you;

b) your managers and employees comply with the SRA's regulatory arrangements which apply to them;

c) your managers and interest holders and those you employ or contract with do not cause or substantially contribute to a breach of the SRA's regulatory arrangements by you or your managers or employees;

d) your compliance officers are able to discharge their duties under rules 9.1 and 9.2 below.

2.2 You keep and maintain records to demonstrate compliance with your obligations under the SRA's regulatory arrangements.

2.3 You remain accountable for compliance with the SRA's regulatory arrangements where your work is carried out through others, including your managers and those you employ or contract with.

2.4 You actively monitor your financial stability and business viability. Once you are aware that you will cease to operate, you effect the orderly wind-down of your activities.

2.5 You identify, monitor and manage all material risks to your business, including those which may arise from your connected practices.

Draft SRA Authorisation of Firms Rules

Part 5: Succession, loss of eligibility and temporary emergency authorisation

14.1 If the last remaining legally qualified manager of an authorised body whose role ensures the body's compliance with the eligibility requirements for its authorisation under rule 1:

a) is sentenced to imprisonment;

b) becomes unable to carry on their role because of incapacity;

c) abandons the business;

d) is made subject to a restriction, condition or other regulatory decision by the SRA or another regulatory body which would prevent or restrict them acting as a manager,

the body must inform the SRA within seven days of becoming aware of the relevant event and, within 28 days of becoming aware of the event, must either become eligible for authorisation (without reference to the manager in question), or cease to carry on reserved legal activities and to hold themselves out as an authorised body.

14.2 Subject to any prescribed application requirements, the SRA may:

a) transfer a body's authorisation to another body where the first body ceases to exist and the second body succeeds to the whole or substantially the whole of its business;

b) substitute a body's authorisation for another type of authorisation where it is satisfied that the body is materially carrying on the same practice, notwithstanding a change in its management or control; and

c) permit any person previously approved as a manager, owner or compliance officer of the body to continue to act in their designated role, notwithstanding the transfer or substitution.

Temporary emergency authorisation or approval

15.1 An application for temporary emergency authorisation may be made:

    a)   within seven days of any change in the management or control of an authorised body which brings into being a new unauthorised body or practice;

    b)   within 28 days of the death or incapacity of a sole practitioner by a solicitor or REL who is:

        (i)   the sole practitioner's executor, personal representative, attorney under a lasting power of attorney, or Court of Protection deputy (as appropriate),

        (ii) a practice manager appointed by the sole practitioner's executor, personal representative, attorney under a lasting power of attorney, or Court of Protection deputy (as appropriate), or

        (iii) an employee of the practice.

15.2 An application for temporary emergency approval of a compliance officer may be made within seven days of an authorised body ceasing to have a COLP or COFA whose designation is approved under Part 4.

15.3 The SRA will only grant an application under rule 15.1(a) or 15.2 if it is satisfied that:

    a)   the body or its managers could not reasonably have commenced a substantive application for authorisation under Part 2 in advance of the events giving rise to the application;

    b)   in relation to an application under rule 15.1(a) the body meets the eligibility requirements under rule 1.1 and will comply with our regulatory arrangements as they apply to authorised bodies;

    c)   in relation to an application under rule 15.2, it has no reason to believe that the individual to which the application relates is not fit and proper to be a compliance officer of the authorised body.

15.4 Temporary emergency authorisation or approval:

    a)   shall be granted for an initial period of 28 days from the date specified;

    b)   may be extended for such period as the SRA thinks fit;

    c)   shall be extended, if a substantive application for authorisation or approval is made during the period of temporary emergency authorisation or approval, pending determination of the substantive application;

    d)   may be revoked or withdrawn, or made subject to such conditions as the SRA considers appropriate, in the public interest;

save that, if the SRA grants temporary emergency authorisation under rule 15.1(b), the authorisation will be deemed to run from the date of death or incapacity and will cease to have effect on the earliest of the date of the winding up of the estate or 12 months from the date of death or incapacity.

Apportionment of periodical fees on succession

16.1 An authorised body which:

    a)   has taken over the whole or a part of one or more authorised bodies; or

    b)   has split or ceded part of its practice to another authorised body and wishes the SRA to take this into account in determining its periodical fee;

must within 28 days of the change taking place deliver to the SRA a notice in the prescribed form.

B2   Useful contact details

LawCare

LawCare helps and supports individual lawyers who are finding it hard to cope with the stresses of practice or life. LawCare also promotes good mental health and wellbeing in the legal community throughout the UK, Ireland, Isle of Man and Jersey.

LawCare does this in four ways.

1. **Confidential helpline – 0800 279 6888**
   Lawyers are supported through a confidential helpline, which is operated by LawCare staff who are all solicitors with experience of practice. The helpline is open Monday to Friday 9 am–7.30 pm and 10 am–4 pm on weekends and bank holidays. It helps anyone in the legal profession who is feeling the pressure of work or study, experiencing relationship or financial problems, or coping with problems related to illness, dependency, bereavement, anxiety, stress or depression.

   Callers are given emotional support and a listening ear. Where further help is required, they can be signposted to other professionals or agencies. Where ongoing support is needed a caller can, if he or she wishes, be referred to a peer supporter. These are lawyer volunteers who have experienced, for example, stress, depression or addiction problems, and therefore have a unique understanding of it.

   LawCare support covers a lawyer's entire practising life, from pre-qualification to retirement. Family members or colleagues can also ring LawCare if they have concerns about someone who they believe is suffering mental health problems.

2. **Information – www.lawcare.org.uk/information-and-support**
   LawCare has a range of factsheets on its website that provide help on many subjects including:

   - Alcohol
   - Anxiety
   - Bullying in the workplace
   - Depression
   - Drugs
   - Sleep problems
   - Moving on from the legal profession
   - Bereavement

   These are available to read online or to download.

3. **Raising awareness**
   Stress continues to be by far the most common reason for callers to contact LawCare. With this in mind, LawCare actively encourages firms to think about and adopt policies which support good mental health and the wellbeing of staff. It also encourages individuals to adopt healthy lifestyles and embrace wellbeing as integral to working effectively as a lawyer.

4. **Tackling stigma**

   LawCare is active in encouraging the profession to talk openly about mental health problems, to reduce the stigma that continues to attach to many conditions. LawCare's website carries the individual stories of lawyers who have been prepared to come forward and talk openly about their personal experience of coping with poor mental health. For those experiencing similar problems the message is: you are not alone.

The Solicitors Regulation Authority

The Cube
199 Wharfside Street
Birmingham B1 1RN
DX: 720293 BIRMINGHAM 47

Contact Centre

Tel: 0370 606 2555

Professional Ethics Helpline

Tel: 0370 606 2577

Email: professional.ethics@sra.org.uk

The Law Society

113 Chancery Lane
London WC2A 1PL
Tel: 020 7242 1222
Fax: 020 7831 0344
DX: 56 London/Chancery Lane

Practice Advice Service

Tel: 020 7320 5675

Email: practiceadvice@lawsociety.org.uk

The Information Commissioner's Office

The Information Commissioner's Office can offer guidance on data protection issues.

Information Commissioner's Office
Wycliffe House
Water Lane
Wilmslow
Cheshire SK9 5AF
Tel: 0303 123 1113

There is an email form on their website at **www.ico.org.uk/global/contact-us/email**.